CANTERBURY
BEFORE THE NORMANS

CANTERBURY
BEFORE THE NORMANS

DAVID BIRMINGHAM

First published in 2015 by Palatine Books,
Carnegie House,
Chatsworth Road
Lancaster LA1 4SL
www.palatinebooks.com

Copyright © David Birmingham

British Library Cataloguing-in-Publication data
A catalogue record for this book is available from the British Library

Paperback ISBN 978-1-910837-01-6

Designed and typeset by Carnegie Book Production

Printed and bound by Nicholson Bass, Belfast, Northern Ireland

CONTENTS

PREFACE

THIS BOOK is based on the work of a whole generation of scholars, authors and archaeologists who have been my literary companions as I attempted to understand the early history of the community in which I live. I am extremely grateful to all of them and hope they will recognise the value of their uncited work despite any distortions I may have introduced. The roots of the project lie far away in Africa where I spent some years trying to interpret early history – the agricultural revolution, the Iron Age, the coming of literacy. This African work involved the interpretation of material culture, the study of comparative linguistics, the grasp of social anthropology, and the use of early church records and of creative historical fiction. In retirement I have enjoyed applying this experience to a different but curiously similar society. The most extensive corpus of data on the material culture of Canterbury and its interpretation is to be found in the publications of the Canterbury Archaeological Trust. The writings, lectures and guided walks of Paul Bennett and his evolving team of thirty-odd archaeological colleagues form the essential underpinning of this book. The popularising interpretations, and any scholarly misinterpretations, are my own stumbling effort. The speculation concerning the 'Celtic' age in Kent owes much to the work of Peter Beresford Ellis. For a local Kentish insight into the Roman world the Historic England guide to Lullingstone Roman villa is richly illustrated and the Canterbury Roman Museum is a gem. Many books about Caesar and Claudius might have been consulted but the one which fortuitously came to hand was by John Peddie. The arrival in Kent of the 'Jutes' and the study of their place in the wider history of the Saxon world is reliant on the work of the late A.M.Everitt and the more recent scholarship of Stuart Brookes and Sue Harrington. Frank Jessup once produced a useful historical atlas of Kent and more recently John Williams and his colleagues have published a wide-ranging volume on Kent before AD 800 which has an extensive bibliography. The work of one outstanding historian of Canterbury, Marjorie Lyle, includes some vivid historical fiction. Some other works which have been consulted are listed at the end of this volume. This book would never have seen the light of day had it not been for the meticulous structural and stylistic editing of Doreen Rosman. It is dedicated to my wife, Elizabeth, whose archaeological work in the Forest of Blean makes excellent use of divining rods.

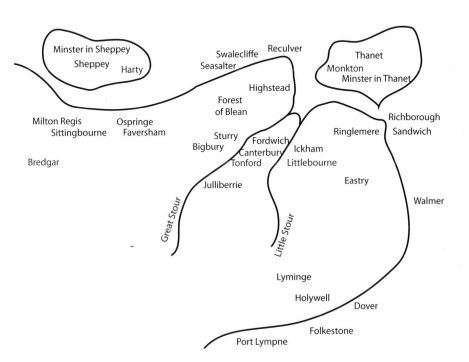

Minster in Sheppey
Sheppey   Harty

Swalecliffe   Reculver
Seasalter

Thanet
Monkton
Minster in Thanet

Highstead

Forest
of Blean

Richborough
Sandwich

Milton Regis   Ospringe
Sittingbourne   Faversham

Ringlemere

Sturry   Fordwich
Bigbury   Canterbury   Ickham
                Tonford   Littlebourne

Bredgar

Julliberrie

Eastry

Walmer

Great Stour

Little Stour

Lyminge

Holywell

Dover

Port Lympne   Folkestone

East Kent before the Normans

PART ONE

THE EARLY ANCESTORS

THE PERMANENT human occupation of Kent began at the end of the most recent Ice Age, some 10,000 years ago. Before that various species of human beings, including the Neanderthals, stretching back over nearly a million years, spasmodically roamed the landscape that later became Britain. When a weather cycle was favourable and the climate was mild, people spread north following any wild game they could hunt. When Arctic conditions reached southward once more, in the regular phases of glacial and inter-glacial climate change, the bands of hunter-gatherers were forced to retreat back into France and towards the warmer Mediterranean. Some of these early predecessors were famous for their fashioning of the heavy hand axes of the Old Stone Age. They left a few traces of their residence around Canterbury and some tools and chippings have been discovered on the river bank a mile or two down-stream from the future city. The 'Acheulian' tool type, dating back a quarter of a million years, was first noted in Europe on the banks of the Somme in France but is also extensively found in parts of Kent.

When the last Ice Age retreated, Kent gradually acquired its recognisable geographical layout. At the same time new deciduous forests of birch, oak, elm, alder, ash and lime spread into the open tundra to join the coppices of holly and pine. The melting of the ice unlocked quantities of water which flooded the great North Sea plains and the islands of the Dogger Bank which had until then linked Britain to Holland and Denmark. Kent was eventually separated from the continent about nine thousand years ago when the waters rose to a point where the waves cut under the white cliffs of Calais and created the English Channel opposite Dover. The important island of Thanet, made of high chalk with a clay cap, survived the rising waters. Many coastal areas, by contrast, including the Romney Flats and the Wantsum Channel, remained flooded throughout the New Stone Age, the Bronze Age and the Iron Age. It was not until after the Roman era that they began to silt up and become medieval sheep pastures or corn fields resembling later Dutch polders.

To obtain a lively account of Stone Age life in the environs of Canterbury one might turn to fictional writing rather than to historians. In his novel *The Gift of Stones* Jim Crace visualises a Stone Age community which looked out to sea from uplands which might have been near Canterbury. The gift of stones which the men possessed was the ability to knap flints, to make knives which could slice meat, scrapers which could clean pelts, sickles which could harvest seeds, harpoons to spear fish, arrows to shoot birds and adzes to fashion wood. The stonewrights in the novel were not great warriors, however, and were constantly threatened by neighbours who raided their flint yards. The robbers were unable to fashion their own flint tools. Amateur stone-knappers did not recognise the optimum materials needed and tried to make tools from riverside mudstone rather than quarrying flints out of chalk mines where the stone had not been fractured and crazed by frost damage. Once brought to the surface, flint could be split, worked, and fitted with handles tied with animal tendons. Flint-knappers sold their wares to flint-mongers from far and wide. There was a good market for tools and weapons among woodsmen and hunters occupying sandy soils across the breadth of Britain.

One site of human activity in the Canterbury countryside which has received close attention is at Highstead, in a parish seven miles north-east of the city, looking out from a low plateau across the Wantsum Channel. The community activities on the site span many centuries and are important in the archaeological history of Britain. As the cold weather retreated northward, hunters of the Middle Stone Age roamed across the clay-capped gravel, scattering abundant butchering implements and other chipped flint tools. When the concept of farming arrived, six or so thousand years ago, people started to enhance their local diet of carefully collected wild seeds by planting, and then harvesting, selected varieties of seed. Agriculture and vegeculture had been independently developed in several corners of the globe but it seems almost certain that in order to reach Britain, farming was slowly taught from neighbour to neighbour across the span of Europe or around its coasts. It is possible that domestic animals may have been adopted before domestic plants. Both may have first been recognised as a valuable addition to a subsistence economy by partially settled peoples who had access to fishing resources along rivers and on coastlines. The 'Neolithic' ideas of the New Stone Age may have spread up the Atlantic coast towards Britain. People who scavenged for shellfish and trawled the coasts and waterways were less mobile than hunters and more capable of adopting a fixed abode suitable for farming. The traditions adopted for early farm-working in Kent were modelled on the traditions developed in Asia Minor and in the Fertile Crescent surrounding the deserts of Syria. The spread of the radical idea of plant and animal domestication involved some degree of migration as well as of learning. The animals like the cereals, adopted in Kent were not local but alien. Wild boars and hinds remained wild, while domestic livestock arrived with wandering herdsmen, seeking the best summer-and-winter pastures and the most reliable springs. Goats, pigs and cattle were introduced to Kent before the end of the Stone Age, though domesticated fowl, hens, ducks and geese may have been later arrivals. Such a scenario would explain how it is that the DNA of Kentish people appears to resemble that of the coastal people of northern Spain. The new ranchers may have come to outnumber the old hunters. When Neolithic agriculture reached the farmlands around Canterbury four thousand years before Christ, some tools became more precise, with polished cutting edges for digging gardens and harvesting crops. Worn flint hoes and sickles could be replaced in Kent by flaking and polishing new local stone cores and then hafting them with glued handles. Butchering tools became more refined as domesticated animals began to supplement the hunted meat obtained from hares or deer, making the need for good equipment greater.

One remarkable archaeological site in the Canterbury district has been locally known since the sixteenth century as 'Julliberrie's grave', the Barrow of Julius, the most famous figure in local antiquity. It is a Neolithic long barrow five miles up river from Canterbury near to the great watermill at Chilham built by Kentish farmers on a high bank silhouetted against the skyline. A length of one hundred and fifty feet of the barrow which is forty feet wide and six feet high is still intact but the other half of it has been quarried away and is now a cottage garden. Since East Kent, unlike West Kent, has few Stonehenge-type sarcen stones suitable for rock tombs, the barrow consisted of a chalk pit surrounded by ditches and covered with mounds of turf. No human bones have been found but one excavation uncovered a fine Scandinavian-type Neolithic tool. In view of its closeness to the European mainland, it is likely that the site was of early agricultural importance, and features on the slope above the barrow suggest that ploughing had taken place, perhaps by 3000 BC. Whatever the original ritual importance of the barrow it probably continued to inspire awe over scores of generations. When the Romans later colonised the Stour valley they too chose this high bank as a suitable burial site. Like their Neolithic ancestors the Romano-British river-dwellers lacked monumental stones and so built funerary cairns with flints. Offerings were later made on the site with shells, pots and even coins.

The Neolithic herdsmen and planters of the New Stone Age continued to exploit suitable soils around Canterbury until new ideas, new technologies and new patterns of habitation were adopted. This transformation was associated with the slow but revolutionary introduction into the community of metal-based technologies. The first metal which gradually but radically modified the economy of Kent over the last two-and-a-half thousand years before Christ was bronze. Pure copper had been used by some Late Stone Age peoples, such as the Iceman who herded sheep in the Austrian Alps around 3000 BC, but the metal age in Britain was essentially based on copper alloys such as bronze and developed a little later. Some of the Bronze Age people who selected fertile tracts of land in the environs of Canterbury were immigrants who had crossed the English Channel. Others were men and women of Kent who were able to adopt the new metalworking crafts and recognise the advantages which bronze tools, and more especially weapons, represented. Bronze tools, unlike flint ones, could be constantly sharpened rather than discarded. Broken tools (unlike stone implements) were never discarded but could be melted down and re-cast. Their efficiency led to some intensification of land-use. Communities could settle in more permanent homesteads or hamlets located in well-chosen settings and stronger tools meant that farmers could dig deeper wells and so use choice stretches of land that had no streams.

Flourishing communities needed not only efficient technology but also good protection against wild beasts or hostile neighbours. Since the Canterbury district had little good stone for building walls, a tradition developed in which earth banks were built, and defensive ditches were dug, to surround habitations, gardens and stock-pens. Bank-and-ditch boundaries demarcating property became key features of the landscape. On open ground residual earth-bank features can be discerned in aerial photographs and in recent years 'lidar' photographs have been able to determine old habitation enclosures and ditch fortifications by electronically penetrating tree cover.

Throughout the history of Canterbury (and its environs) questions arise about the purpose of labour-intensive buildings, be they earth banks, or later walls of imported stone and towers of baked bricks. Military interpretations are usually the first explanation adopted. The importance of building works to symbolise power and prestige has, however, an equally long history. The monumental architecture of both Roman and Norman colonisers was impressive as they imposed their might on the indigenous peoples. In a similar vein some Bronze Age enclosures might be interpreted in political and symbolic terms, rather than only as kraals to keep sheep and oxen safe from wolves or cattle thieves. One enclosure on the Highstead site might have been a 'mini hill fort' which symbolised the power of a clan leader. It could equally have been a military bastion from which sentinels with a view down to the sea could warn the community of impending danger. Such enclosures might also have provided a rudimentary refuge in times of trouble with the neighbours or invaders.

One of the enclosures at Highstead held a farmhouse and a farmyard protected by a ditch-and-mound on top of which a hedge may have been planted. The four gateways were closed off at night with wooden hurdles. This compound measured more than 100 feet across and appeared to include two round huts on the western side and pens for livestock on the eastern side. Although bones survive poorly in local soils, enough have been found to suggest that Late Bronze Age people reared the first horses to arrive in Kent. Some of the finest technical work carried out at Highstead was the making of bronze shoulder pins to fasten woven cloaks and dresses. Fragments of clay moulds into which molten bronze could be poured to make these clothing pins have been found in an 'industrial' enclosure. To make bronze more fluid and malleable, later smiths added not only eight per cent of tin to their copper but also three per cent of lead. It is likely that the local coppersmiths also cast spear-heads which could be sharpened and polished with whetstones and one such spear has been found in the old drove road, the Radfall, which crosses the Forest of Blean, just north of Canterbury. Even more impressive is a 'hoard' of bronze dating from about 800 BC which was buried in Bogshole Lane between Canterbury and Whitstable.

This find included eleven broken bronze axes as well as two spear-heads; the burying of such broken tools may have had a ritual significance. Alternatively the hoard may have simply been hidden scrap metal awaiting future use when a better proportion of hardening tin could be added.

Metal-working, and metal trading, were at the top end of Bronze Age industrial and commercial activity. But a more extensive productive activity concerned objects made of clay. In contrast to metal objects, ceramic objects were heavy in relation to their value and so less attractive to long-distance merchants. Early bronze-using migrants seem to have greatly valued ceramic wares known to archaeologists as 'beakers'. The beakers may have been prestigious objects of veneration rather than every-day table-ware. In the days when migration was deemed to be the main method of cultural diffusion scholars even dubbed the pot-makers the 'Beaker People'. The learning of ceramic skills, however, did not necessarily involve population movement and at Highstead local people learned to manufacture the range of Bronze Age ceramics – jars, pots, bowls and cups – using local clays. Ceramic ideas and fashions readily crossed frontiers and coastlines. The makers of Bronze Age pottery learnt their style of ceramic craftsmanship from one another across the whole span of Europe 4000 years ago. By the end of the Bronze Age cross-channel trade had increased to such an extent that pottery merchants were not only adopting new continental styles but were also importing finished ceramic wares. The dissemination of costly objects represents the growth of trade in centuries long before the invention of coinage, while 'gift exchanges' between élite families, possibly on the occasion of high-status marriages, enhanced the long-distance flow of goods. Influential 'Big Men', with high-status connections, flourished in Kent after the Highstead community had been dispersed. Inside ditch-and-bank compounds chieftains lived in round houses quite unlike the old Neolithic long huts. One such farming complex has been excavated behind Herne Bay railway station and another lies on a bluff above the coast at nearby

Swalecliffe. At Holywell Coombe (on the southern foothills of the North Downs) some fifteen miles out of Canterbury, the ceramic vessels on the Bronze Age farms were decorated with comb marks on the reddish shards. These farms used ploughs and the marks of an 'ard' ploughshare can be detected, and since ploughs are most efficiently drawn by oxen, the Holywell farmers must have trained draft animals. They also butchered domestic animals including pigs.

The eating habits of the people of the Canterbury district continued to include much food gathered from the wild, as in Neolithic times, and many local culinary traditions carried through until the Roman era. Game which had long been familiar continued to be hunted after domesticated mammals had begun to supply alternative sources of meat. The snaring of hares was relatively easy but the shooting of fleet-footed deer required real skill and gave hunters high social status. Wealthy people prized foods rich in protein while lesser folk continued to develop skills in selecting any wild food of any quality if it contributed to survival. Snails were one of the most easily 'hunted' forms of protein as they have remained in many parts of the world until the present day. A more specialised way of gathering richly nutritious food was by harvesting seashore crustaceans such as limpets, winkles and mussels. Oysters were widely gathered and long remained cheap and nutritious until recently becoming specialised and expensive. The importance of river fish to the Stour-side people of prehistoric Canterbury is not fully recorded since fish bones do not survive well, but as the river is rich in eels as well as pike, roach, perch, trout and even carp it must be assumed that fish was traditionally eaten from an early date. Fisher-folk may have cured some of their catch by drying, or salting, or smoking it for sale inland to communities which had neither streams nor ponds. Rivers and marshes were also important breeding grounds for waterfowl. Many types of bird could be captured for food and the eggs of any wild bird could be eaten. The large eggs from water-side nests must have been especially prized. Beyond the rivers and coastal marshes lay the deep sea. The extent of early sea-fishing, or shoreline fish-trapping, requires further study but weights of stone, and even of lead, were used over time to sink fishing nets. Fish caught around the coast included herring, cod, mackerel, conger eel, ray, gurnard, garfish and sea bream.

Bronze Age communities trained more efficient craftspeople than their ancestors. A good coppersmith needed not only a plentiful supply of charcoal, but also wide contacts to obtain the raw material for forging tools, weapons and ornaments. In Kent (as in the rest of Europe) metallurgists moved fairly rapidly from using pure copper to using copper alloys. The most important of the new alloy ingredients was tin, a relatively scarce metal. The communities around what later became the city of Canterbury could purchase tin or ready-smelted copper but bronze alloy was usually traded as finished ingots or as recycled scrap metal. One long-distance sea route brought tin from the Cornish mines. A wreck found off the coast of south Devon by metal detectorists was that of a small boat, made of hides stretched over a wooden frame, carrying not only ingots but also weapons and ornaments. Kent coppersmiths also traded scrap metal with their neighbours in France and Belgium.

In addition to the evidence of sea trade, there is some evidence for overland trade with the west following paths on the high ground out of the Stour Valley. These tracks (used two thousand years later by religious pilgrims wanting to reach Canterbury) may originally have served as routes for taking much prized salt from the coastal pans to inland communities. Brine baths for drying such salt were in use on the seashore flats of the north Canterbury coast in locations bearing such revealing names as Seasalter. Salt, important in any diet, was used to preserve both meat and fish as a relish for consumers who were by now eating meals consisting of more harvested corn and less roast game. The salt tracks may also have been used to bring minerals into the Stour valley.

The extent of Bronze Age trading, or exchange, can be illuminated by discoveries made in funeral barrows excavated at Monkton, across the Wantsum Channel. In their funerary rituals Late Bronze

Age people decorated their tombs. The tenderness which such people felt for their loved ones is perhaps best illustrated by a Scottish grave in which a bouquet of meadowsweet was placed in a stone coffin 4000 years ago. On the continent the graves of great leaders were furnished with weapons – breast-plates, helmets, shields and swords which commemorated a man's status as well as his military prowess. Such objects were probably also made in Kent, as were copper bracelets and perforated clay cups which might have been used for burning incense. Other goods with which Kentish people furnished tombs included disc beads made of black jet which had been quarried from the cliffs of Whitby in Yorkshire. Another costly votive offering was a funerary urn which had been brought all the way from Cornwall. Even more exotic were imported pieces of tin-glazed faïence from France. The telling evidence of long-distance trade supplying Kentish communities is also provided by the presence of amber objects in Bronze Age graves. This fossilized resin probably came from the seabed of the Baltic beyond northern Germany. Affinities with the sea are also indicated by a Thanet grave which was decorated with a whale bone.

The existence of long-distance transport can be supported by a discovery in a silted-up creek at Dover. The Bronze Age boat which came to rest in the Dover creek was a heavy seagoing vessel nearly forty feet long and capable of carrying several tons of cargo. It was made of thick planks slotted and wedged together and then tightly sewn with twisted withies of yew sapling. The complex joints of the finished boat were caulked with moss and beeswax, making a vessel quite capable of crossing the English Channel in 1550 BC. With such a vessel the spread of ideas, fashions, foods, clothing, pottery – and possibly also trade languages – could have passed from continental Europe to off shore Britain with few problems. The Dover Bronze Age boat was also used for coastal trading along the southern shore of Britain and some of the sand found in the boat had piggy-backed into Kent from a beach in Dorset. Travelling west beyond Dorset to the copper mines of Devon and to the even more valuable tin mines of Cornwall was readily feasible. Since the architects of Kent, then as later, often had to rely on soft chalk blocks and small flint pebbles as their local building material it is possible that a boat like the Dover Boat may have been used to carry cut blocks of limestone or sandstone as one of its pay-loads. Two thousand years later building stone was being imported into Kent by sea, this time for the building of Canterbury's great Norman cathedral. Once the long-distance cargoes had arrived in Dover they may have been divided up into smaller consignments for delivery by little boats to the creek-side harbours of the Wantsum Channel or even up the Stour to quayside settlements near Canterbury.

An imaginative account of the building of the Dover Bronze Age boat has been written by Peter Clark of the Canterbury Archaeological Trust. Once he had grasped the significance of the technical skills involved in crafting a sea-going vessel with bronze tools, he and his team set about building a replica, shown in exhibitions in Belgium and France as well as at Dover. The original boat, preserved with the technical help of the Mary Rose Trust, is to be seen in the Dover museum. Peter Clark's account of Bronze Age boat building runs as follows. Each tall straight oak used to build the boat was three hundred years old when felled and had a girth of eleven feet, a giant such as has long since vanished from the forests of western Europe. Small bronze axes weighing about a kilogram were used to fell each tree and then to split the trunk into three planks, each weighing ten tons. The green wood was too dense to be floated down a river and had to be dragged through the forest to the coast. The fashioning of the boat was a task undertaken by itinerant specialist carpenters, craftsmen who were held in almost religious awe for their skill in assessing the seafaring needs and opportunities of each community they visited. When completed the forty-foot boat was seven feet wide and two feet deep, no mere dugout but a sophisticated sea-going vessel to be launched with great ceremony and celebration. Once on the water its mixed cargo included foodstuffs, textiles, quern-stones, shale, jet, jewellery and most important of all bronze. Peter Clark concludes his essay by

In 1992 a Bronze Age boat, made of oak planks, was discovered in Dover. Around 1550 BC this huge vessel had carried pay loads along the coast of England and across the Channel. © Canterbury Archaeological Trust Ltd

saying that the boat was also 'a vehicle for social and political inter-course with other communities both nearby and far away. It carried gifts, news, dowries, tribute, emissaries, brides, stories and religion'.

Bronze Age sea-trading may have been large in scale but it was not altogether new. A thousand years or so before the Bronze Age boat was abandoned at Dover, the Canterbury district was already in commercial contact with the continental mainland. A community of Neolithic farmers had acquired a very fine ceremonial hand-axe which was preserved in a pristine state, probably as homage to the gods of good weather, rich fertility and fine crops. The Canterbury axe is now a prized item in the British Museum. It is made of fine greenish jade, a stone which takes a good polished finish, and the raw block from which this British polished axe was made had been quarried in the Dolomite outriders of the Alps in northern Italy. The trade routes used by Neolithic pack animals and sea-merchants to bring such treasured items to Canterbury cannot yet be plotted. There is a suggestion, however, that the chipping of the stone core, and the fashioning of the axe shape, may have taken place not in Britain but in Brittany, on the coast of France. The historic links between Brittany and Cornwall are well-known, since in more recent times the people on both these sets of rocky promontories jutting out into the Atlantic have spoken closely related 'Celtic' languages. Merchant contacts between Cornwall and Brittany could have pre-dated the discovery and exploitation of the British mines which supplied tin to the Bronze Age civilisations of the Mediterranean. A sea-lane, on the evidence of the Canterbury axe, must have been much older than the route used by the Bronze Age vessel found at Dover.

The Canterbury district was not only noted for its Neolithic *objets d'art* like the jade axe and for its strategic weapons made of copper alloys. The local Bronze Age people also knew how to work gold and where to obtain it. European gold is not found in abundance and early British gold probably came from the remote hard-rock districts of Wales and Ireland. Gold dust, washed from streams, would have been packed in cattle horns, carefully concealed in leather pouches, and carried by merchants travelling in well-protected foot caravans. Small quantities of gold had long been used for making brooches and rings which symbolised status in societies across the ages. As early as the middle Bronze Age, however, one graveyard near Canterbury used gold on a much more lavish scale to celebrate the power of the divine. In place of great megaliths, such as those rolled on to Salisbury Plain to build Stonehenge, the men and women of Kent commemorated the prowess of their ancestors by worshipping a fine gold cup placed on a shrine located at Ringlemere Farm some ten miles out of Canterbury. The gold cup is extremely beautiful in spite of being badly dented when a modern plough struck it while cultivating the field in which it had become buried. It is about six inches tall and is made to look like a small bowl of 'corded ware' (a coiled clay vessel). It appears to be a votive offering placed in a holy place which had been the site of burial barrows with their origin in the third millennium BC.

Ringlemere was originally an earthen 'henge', a circular compound comparable to the stone henges and wooden henges found elsewhere in southern Britain. The site was still prominent in later years when Bronze Age peoples built barrow mounds inside the enclosure. It was into such a barrow that the gold cup was buried, possibly around 2000 BC. The only British cup of comparable size and worth was found in the west country and the Ringlemere cup could have been imported from the west rather than from the continent, though local Bronze Age smiths may have been capable of fashioning their own gold objects using heated crucibles. Such a goldsmithing tradition certainly developed in Kent two thousand years later when the craftfolk of Faversham became noted for their skills in the metal-work associated with jewellery-making. Fortunately the Ringlemere cup was rescued from further plough damage by a careful metal detectorist. It is now in the British Museum which paid a quarter of a million pounds sterling for the privilege of exhibiting it among its greatest treasures.

Gold was the first and finest of the metals but a far more important one was iron. It was iron which democratised metal use for the common husbandman and housewife. The adoption of iron as a revolutionary technology was not an obvious step. Iron, unlike copper, did not appear to be shiny and beautiful when smelted. The making of iron was not an intuitive evolution but rather something that required a 'magical' element as well as high furnace temperatures. In other parts of the world the secret craft was monopolised by men to the ritual exclusion of women. The huge advantage of iron over copper, however, was that the raw ore was widely available in Kent. Flows of slag waste are readily found in the woods

In 2014 Bronze Age tools were used to construct a reduced-sized replica of the Dover boat, which was tested at sea and competed in the great London river race.
© Canterbury Archaeological Trust Ltd

around Canterbury where ironsmiths once worked. The first stage of iron- working produces a molten black slag, which was thrown away, and left ugly 'cauliflower' lumps of iron 'bloom'. Only after the first, laborious, stage of smelting was completed could the iron be re-heated and then beaten into a useable form that served for tool-making. Unlike coppersmiths, the blacksmiths were not able to heat their metal to a sufficient temperature to make it molten in order to fashion cast iron utensils. To make tools with hard edges blacksmiths heated, forged and beat iron in which a small compo-nent of carbon had been retained. Initially the strength of iron made it valuable for making small rivets to fix handles on elegant bronze swords, but later enough good sword iron became available

The Canterbury jade axe, a highly-polished ritual object from the Neolithic period, was made out of stone quarried in the Italian Dolomites. © The Trustees of the British Museum

to make whole blades. As iron became increasingly affordable its use spread from symbolic weapons to functional ones and then to such everyday objects as cleavers for butchers, axes for foresters, or hoes for farmers. Equally important was the development of wood-working tools – hammers, rasps, saws, files, adzes, chisels, indeed all the tool-kit of a modern carpenter with the exception of the screwdriver. One of the most mundane but useful of the Iron Age inventions was the iron nail, sometimes up to a foot long, which could be used for building houses, boats and fortified palisades.

The heartland of the Western European Iron Age was in the Alps. It was from the salt-mining community of Hallstadt or comparable sites in Austria that Early Iron Age technology and craftsmanship spread towards the English Channel. And it was among the lake-dwelling communities of La Tène in Switzerland that the later refinement of fine arts and Iron Age rituals gained their name. These Alpine sites were not just famous for the nurturing of iron technologies, but were also the Western cradle of 'Celtic' culture, one homeland of the 'Celtic' peoples of the Classical Age. The term 'Celt' was originally a derogatory name used for the northern neighbours of Greece's great Mediterranean trading empire. The term later came to be applied to almost any of the peoples who lived outside the sphere of Mediterranean influence. Comparison has been made with the term 'Indian' which Columbus applied to the Caribbean islanders but which later spread to be applied to all the indigenous peoples of both North and South America. Eventually 'Celtic' cultures and languages were introduced to communities as far afield as the 'Galatian' villages of Asia Minor visited by St Paul, through the 'Gaulish' kingdoms of France, to the 'Pays de Galles' in the hills of Wales. 'Celtic' culture in the Iron Age relates primarily to material culture since literacy did not spread far beyond the Mediterranean sphere and so did not preserve the languages of the various peoples known as 'Celts'.

The 'Celtic' dimension of Canterbury's history is shrouded in mystery. The earliest historical writings assume that 'Celtic' languages and cultures were prevalent in Kent during the last centuries before Christ, but the concept of a 'Celtic' people is very hard to define. There were no great waves of 'Celtic' migrants sweeping across the Channel during the Iron Age. On the other hand many

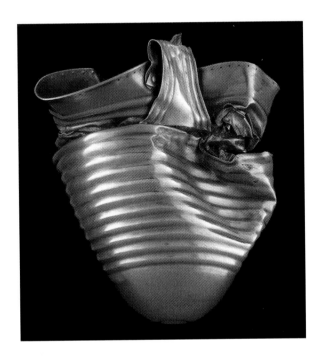

The 'Ringlemere' gold cup, dating from the middle Bronze Age, was found in a ritual site near Canterbury. © The Trustees of the British Museum

17

'Celtic' customs and crafts were adopted in Britain. In western Britain, where they were not later overlain by Roman or Saxon or Norman languages and traditions, a 'Celtic' way of speaking and behaving survived for two or more millennia. In Canterbury the 'Celtic' traditions which spread in from France and Belgium have, in contrast to Wales or Cornwall, only left rather ephemeral clues. The odd place name, such as Durovernon – the river-bank surrounded by alder trees – survived into Roman times and Canterbury's river, the Great Stour, still bears its pre-Roman name. Otherwise we have little idea of how people spoke. 'Celts' did not leave any pictorial evidence let alone written texts. Greek seamen who circumnavigated the British Isles and wrote about them in the fourth century BC were impressed by the fields of corn grown on the Isle of Thanet but told us little about the people. One is tempted to suggest that 'Celtic' vernaculars may have spread into pre-Roman Kent as a *lingua franca* used by merchants in association with Iron Age trade and technology. Many of the underlying cultures, however, appear to have spread up the Atlantic coast from Spain several thousand years earlier.

'Celtic' societies evolved hierarchies of power and status which were most obviously symbolised by the goods placed in the graves of important women and men. Although many iron weapons were functional rather than ritual, in contrast to the fine symbolic bronze swords displayed by earlier noblemen, some iron sword handles were finely decorated with bone, horn, glass and enamel. Status in the house of an Iron Age chieftain was displayed in great feasts. Headmen lubricated their festivals with imported wine as well as with Kentish ales. Households harvested a hundred different edible plants to flavour their meals. Royal cooks roasted meat on iron spits held up to the fireside with great fire-dogs. The fashioning of expensive fireside iron-ware required many hot hours of work at the forge. Iron was of great importance in symbolising wealth and status but so too was fine jewellery which was displayed on festive occasions. The richest of British kings wore 'torc' neck-collars, made with eight-stranded gold wire and decorated with exotic jewels. As power grew leaders began to control a new source of wealth and status in the form of land. It was well-drained, fertile, land which attracted the successive generations of later continental rulers (Italian, German and French) when they aspired to dominate the 'Celtic' lands of Kent during the first millennium after Christ.

Fascinating evidence of an Early Iron Age community has been found north west of Canterbury on the site of the present Kent College. For several centuries settlers occupied land which had previously been worked by Bronze-Age farmers. They built themselves an unusually large 'round house' measuring fifteen metres in diameter. At the neighbouring University of Kent a 2012 excavation, prior to the construction of Turing College, uncovered further Iron-Age occupation from a later period. Some of the finds revealed industrial activity, working metals, textiles and leather. A wooden-lined retting bath suggested the preparation of fibres. Associated commercial importance was revealed by a particularly fine gold 'Stater' coin sifted out of the red mud and dust of the London clay. Timber was apparently plentiful, as shown in charcoal pits, but water less so and one well, still containing its wooden ladder, may have survived from the Bronze Age. The size of the ten-acre site, and the variety of the evidence found, makes it comparable in importance to Highstead, seven miles further north.

As prosperity grew along the Stour Valley the Iron Age community built an impressive fortress at Bigbury, above the bank of the river, overlooking the future city of Canterbury. A great double earth bank surrounded compounds spreading over twenty-five acres. Down the slope on the north side of the hill an ancillary annexe of a further eight acres enjoyed a year-round spring of fresh water. This secondary enclosure would have been ideal for keeping horses. Although the horse may have arrived from the open plains of Ukraine and Hungary in the last years of the Bronze Age, the revolutionary use of horses for both economic and military activity belongs to the heyday of the Iron Age. The Bigbury horses had to be safely coralled near to the main human settlement in case they should suddenly be required in time of war. The hilltop itself had settlements clustered round a water cistern which could keep the community alive even if a military siege temporarily cut the inhabitants off from the springs around the foot of the hill. The geographical scale of the community which centred on Bigbury has not yet been adequately mapped out. The site may have been the centre of a 'Celtic' *oppidum,* or townscape, though not on the scale of the great *oppidum* at Colchester on the opposite side of the Thames. It has been suggested, however, that the overall area of managed farm land might have stretched as far as the next hilltop, at Perry Wood in the west, making the Canterbury rural complex one of the larger, if least studied, of Britain's Iron Age communities. Across a little stream half a mile north of Bigbury a second enclosure, known as Homestall, is no better mapped than Perry Wood but lidar technology scans suggest it could have been twice as large as the Bigbury enclosure. Homestall Hill might have been a large pen for cattle, which were a major source of wealth in Iron Age economies since cows could not only reproduce themselves but could live for up to ten years spanning the fat seasons and the lean. The walls at Homestall may have been as high as the ones at Bigbury but unlike hill forts cut in chalk, which retain their shape, the Canterbury hill forts were built on soils of gravel and sand and were subject to erosion so that the original height of the ramparts is difficult to judge. The banks above the great ditches may have been ten feet tall and were almost impregnable, though not completely so, as the Romans later discovered. The slopes leading up to the forts from both north and south were so steep that they presented a particularly severe challenge to an attacking cavalry. The eastern entrance to the Bigbury enclosure, not far from the zig-zag where a modern road cuts through the fortifications, was presumably barred with heavy-duty timbers of which some post holes can still be traced.

An imaginative account of life at Bigbury has been written by Ron Pepper, a one-time city councillor with a taste for archaeology. He suggests that once a large part of the hilltop had been cleared and fortified at the end of the Iron Age, a community flourished on the site. The *oppidum* may have been used for defence but it was also a highly visible symbol of wealth and power which folk in the valley could see on the skyline. The hilltop settlement may have had a fair-ground and been used for religious festivals, for feasting and for storytelling. Even the limited archaeological exploration so far undertaken has unearthed not only agricultural tools such as ploughs and sickles but also adzes and chisels. The iron kitchen equipment included pot-hooks, tripods, fire dogs and cauldron arms, whilst the importance of horses was revealed not only by the chariot equipment but also by harness fittings and a three-link snaffle bit.

This gold coin, found at the University of Kent, shows that coinage was used in Iron Age Canterbury before the Roman invasion. © Canterbury Archaeological Trust Ltd

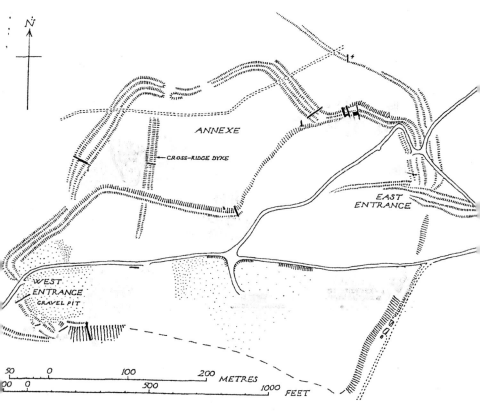

Plan of Bigbury Iron Age hill fort, possibly visited by Caesar in 54 BC.

Timber-framed houses with drip-gully drainage below the thatched eaves had clay floors around the hearth, and a deep communal water cistern with a clay lining that could hold five thousand gallons of captured rain water. Speculation about the commercial importance of Bigbury has focussed on the discovery of some iron slave shackles now held in Manchester museum. These suggest that the eight-acre annexe may have contained a slave compound, a holding pen for war captives awaiting sale on the European slave markets. Since the wealth of the expanding Roman Empire was based on the buying and selling of literally millions of boy and girl slaves it is likely that Kent was known to the slave merchants of the continental mainland and that chained caravans of war-captives and convicts were regularly shipped across the Channel. The Roman author Strabo mentioned slaves, along with corn, cattle, hides and hunting dogs, as important 'commodities' which Romans obtained from Britain, and it seems that in exchange the people of Bigbury imported large amphorae of wine for high days and holidays. On other days their sustenance consisted of spelt wheat, barley and oats as well as nuts, berries, fruit and honey. Together with hunting, fishing and fowling the Bigbury environment offered a good Iron Age living.

Julius Caesar attempted to rubbish the British 'Celts' as 'Barbarians' but other Romans noted their sophistication and their quick intellectual abilities. Cicero reported that their calendar was scientifically superior to the Roman one. Britons, like other 'Celts', had no written records but their intense oral learning meant that laws, rituals and traditions were well preserved. Even Caesar was impressed by the religious roles played by 'Celtic' druids. Bards recited poems and played musical instruments. In matters of law British women had a higher status than those of Rome and were entitled to retain property in their own right when marrying into a polygynous household. Clean and well-dressed British people despised the coarse Roman legions on the continent for the absence of soap in their kit bags. British linen cloaks were fastened with good quality brooches, hair was worn long and stout trousers kept out the winter cold. Men and women of status were known for their ornate necklaces and jewellery held on finely twisted threads of gold. Local coinage was being produced and the military prowess of a chief in his war chariot was stamped on each coin. The 'Celts' particularly valued their horses, and harnesses were finely decorated with coloured enamelling. In order to move foot soldiers and chariots rapidly, whether in local wars on land or to repel sea-borne invaders, the chiefs of Kent built good roads. Unlike the next generation of roads, which the Romans paved with gravel and stone, the old roads were paved with wood when they had to cross marshy ground. These roads could be used not only by two-wheeled chariots but also by pack-horses and transport wagons. 'Celtic' laws governed the maintenance of highways, the laying of brushwood, the mending of bridges, and the building of causeways.

During the last centuries of the Iron Age the future citizens of Canterbury found that the later Castle Street quarter of the city was an attractive location. It lay on higher ground above the marshy banks of the Stour river. The early choice of this site was possibly dictated by the availability of a river ford which led down Water Lane and across the marshes and islands which later became the medieval home to the Franciscan Greyfriars. This ancient crossing led to the prehistoric track-way up to the North Downs. It was in this quarter, which became the heart of the Iron Age 'city', that the Romans later found ground firm enough to build their great multi-storied theatre of baked clay bricks. It was also nearby that the Normans chose to build their great fortress, the castle keep. The evidence relating to the first town dwellers is deeply hidden underneath the layers of subsequent architectural development but ceramic finds provide a rough chronology of cultural evolution. Tall jars were built with rings of hand-coiled clay set on a bed of coarse crushed flint. Bowls of finer ware were made by mixing ground chips of flint with the potting clay to improve the firing. These Stour Valley pots were quite distinct from those being made fifteen miles away on the far side of the Downs. Over time modifications to pottery styles crept seamlessly into Canterbury. The shoulders of pots began to acquire a fashionable 'rusticated' appearance and red and white colouring was used as a finish. Towards the end of the Iron Age, around the time of Christ, a new range of ceramic ware was made in Canterbury as pot-makers replaced the use of flint chips with a new technique which involved recycling old crushed pots to make a powder known as 'grog' and mixing it with fresh clay. This 'grog-tempered' clay was sometimes reinforced with a variety of other materials such as sand, chalk or organic materials like chaff

Fine ceramic ware, made by late Iron Age inhabitants of Canterbury, in imitation of 'Belgic' pots fashioned on the far side of the Channel. © Canterbury Archaeological Trust Ltd

and chopped straw. Most of this pottery was handmade but some plates began to be thrown on a potter's wheel.

Over the last Iron Age centuries Canterbury witnessed changes not only to ceramic and metal-working technologies but also in the domestic economy. Beside the new buildings, underground storage pits for grain were dug and lined with clay as an efficient means of protecting valuable crops from the depredations of rats and mice. Food preservation also required a skilled monitoring of humidity either in ventilated granaries or in air-tight storage pits. Failure could lead to starvation in the next hungry season. The local pottery styles were supplemented by new ones learnt from continental neighbours with new shapes, colouring and decoration, as on Canterbury-fashioned 'Belgic' pots. The old academic idea that great cultural change involved rolling up the population map and re-seeding the land with fresh immigrants has now been discarded. Ties of diplomacy, marriage, commerce and religion would have powerful effects on popular culture without an explanatory need for conquest or migration. In the last few decades before Christ, tableware being imported included cups, bowls, platters, beakers, and flagons, some of Red Samian ware with the fine lustre developed in southern Gaul. Many amphorae wine jars have also been found in pre-Roman layers of city deposits.

The evidence of extensive trade between Canterbury and the continent is clear when the imported fragments are studied. Much more difficult is the study of exports. The lack of any language evidence in Britain means that one is dependent on the records from the mainland where Latin was spreading into use. Corn and hides are mentioned in the first documentary references but another likely source of foreign exchange was textiles. Although textiles themselves do not survive very well in archaeological deposits, a number of clues can be found. Sheep-rearing had been an important Kent industry since Neolithic times and spindle whorls, used for centuries before the invention of the spinning wheel, took on new conical shapes rather than cylindrical shapes of earlier times. Loom weights used to keep the threads taut on a hanging loom also evolved as the industry flourished. Traders familiar with market conditions in Rome realised that British textiles were greatly appreciated for their quality and for the dyes that were used to give the kilts and togas their brilliant colours. As the trade increased merchants in the 'Celtic' world expanded the use of coinage. Gold coins, invented in Greece and weighing eight grams, began to circulate among 'Celtic' mercenaries who had served in the Greek armies of Philip of Macedonia and of his son Alexander the Great. Over the next three hundred years coins were not only accepted in Iron Age Britain but also imitated there. Local political leaders made their own facsimile coins of silver and bronze before the Roman Empire introduced its widely-recognised international coinage.

Although the history of the Iron Age of Canterbury is still embryonic it is clear that the community was flourishing and it is not therefore surprising that when the Romans arrived they built their key city on the old Iron Age site. For the first four centuries of the Christian calendar Canterbury was an energetic city in constant evolution. Even when the Romans withdrew it was not so very long before the abandoned city revived and, unlike the deserted Roman city of Silchester in Hampshire, Canterbury was re-occupied and built over by Jutes, Saxons and Normans and by their descendants to the present day.

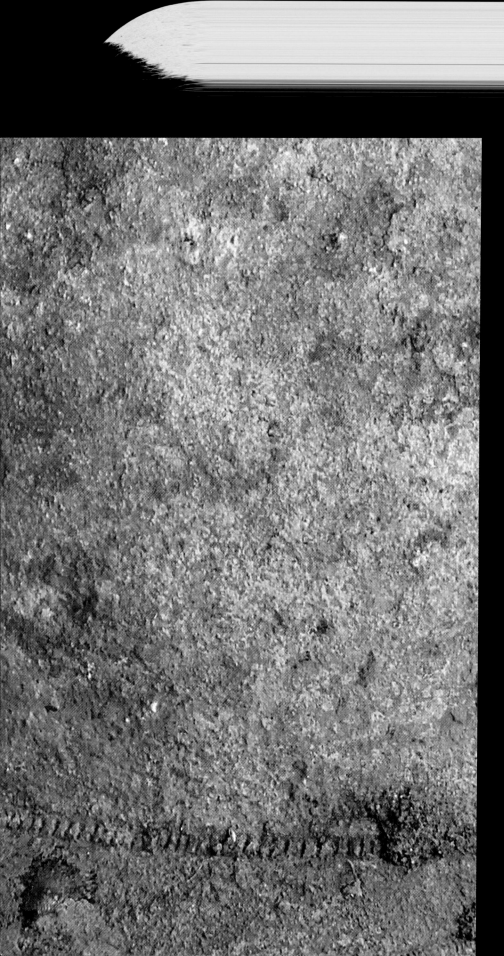

PART TWO

ROMAN SOLDIERS AND SETTLERS

CAESAR'S FIRST foray into Britain in 55 BC had been some years in the planning. The sea merchants of Brittany were concerned by the news of the impending invasion, fearing that a Roman conquest would ruin their independent and profitable trade with the British Isles. Caesar therefore decided to attack Brittany first and pre-empt any possible military alliance the coastal Gauls might make with Britain. He seized eighty sailing ships of their merchant fleet to help carry his invasion force across the Channel. Onto these vessels he loaded his best infantry legions, the VII and the X, each with a strength of 5000 men. He also planned to take eighteen ships of cavalry and 48 oar-driven galleys of fighting auxiliaries. The expedition was due to leave Boulogne for Britain on 24 August but the cavalry ships missed their appointed tide and were delayed. The infantry meanwhile hove to under the South Foreland watched by the British cohorts of charioteers. When the 10,000 Roman infantrymen reached the shallows at Walmer the tide was out and the men had to wade through 200 yards of surf with full packs and sodden uniforms. They were met with volleys of javelins to which they replied with sling-shots. Once they had landed the Romans were surprised by the disciplined chariot charge of an enemy whom they had deceptively been told would be a Barbarian rabble. Once the Romans had regrouped and installed their powerful catapults the battle on the beaches became a stalemate. Truce negotiations were interrupted by a great gale which not only scattered the delayed cavalry but severely damaged many of the infantry's transport ships. Time was now needed to conduct repairs but Caesar had failed to bring adequate rations for his men. He therefore sent them out to forage among crops, loot granaries and rustle cattle. The British forces were able to harass these foraging parties. Although Roman catapults were able to defend the beachhead, Caesar's forces were vulnerable out in the field and the X legion almost suffered the ultimate disgrace of losing its standard to the enemy. After six weeks of skirmishes Caesar was eventually able to withdraw. His reputation was severely tarnished and he faced stern criticism from the Senate at Rome.

Caesar made much more elaborate preparations for his second invasion of Britain in the following year, the one which brought him to Canterbury. After a troubled winter of imperial politics (during which his daughter died and her widowed husband Pompey, challenged his father-in-law in the Senate) Caesar returned to the Channel ports in June 54 BC. On this occasion he had ordered the building of 'hundreds' of shallow-draft transport ships which could land five of his legions and 2000 cavalrymen close inshore at Walmer. This time the army carried enough grain to preclude the need to scatter men across the countryside seeking rations. The fleet arrived at 4 a.m. on July 7 and by noon had landed without resistance. That night, during the third watch, Caesar marched along the twelve-mile road to Canterbury and arrived before dawn at Tonford, the long ford across the Great Stour. The enemy chariots were stationed on the far bank of the river but on seeing the size of the Roman force they appear to have withdrawn. The VII legion crossed the ford and stormed up Bigbury hill to reach the great ramparts with defensive ditches and a palisade topping. The advance was covered by a human wall of shield–bearing soldiers until the sappers could throw up an earthen ramp sufficiently high for the troops to run up it and pour into the enclosure. They found it vacant. After two nights without sleep, one on board ship and one on a night march from Walmer, the Roman force did not have the strength to follow up the capture of Bigbury by chasing the enemy. Before the cavalry could maximise the infantry's initial success, news came from Walmer that once again the Roman fleet had been caught by a severe summer storm. Forty vessels had been wholly wrecked and any soldier with carpentry skills was needed back at the beach to repair the remainder of the fleet. It was ten days before Caesar could return to Canterbury. Meanwhile British troops, including both chariots and cavalry, came down from the Thames along the Kentish roads but their support for the Canterbury resistance was ineffectual. Caesar moved up to the Medway fords torching villages and slaughtering flocks of sheep. The next barrier was the Thames itself where bridges had been destroyed and pikes had been placed in the fords. Still Caesar advanced, capturing slaves as he went. Back in Kent local troops tried without success to storm the Roman landing ground at Walmer. Roman raiding parties then spread out and captured enough marketable slaves to meet the cost of their second British expedition. By the end of September Caesar and his invasion force withdrew back to Gaul with their loot and their prisoners. Initially any thought of a third expedition to Britain was halted by unrest in Gaul and by an uprising in Brittany. Even more serious troubles awaited Caesar in Rome where civil war broke out, pitting him once more against his son-in-law Pompey. The British campaigns had yielded numbers of profitable slaves from Canterbury and beyond but Romans had not reached the British sources of mining wealth. Silver, lead, copper, gold, iron and tin all remained in British hands. Improved access to the industrial markets in spinning, weaving, pottery, leather-working or corn-milling did not outweigh the prospective cost of sending a third invasion force. For the next ninety-odd years Rome traded with Kent and some local rulers may even have paid tribute to the empire, but not until AD 43 did Rome once again think seriously of invading.

Little material evidence exists relating to Caesar's visits to Britain but in 2012 a meticulous metal detectorist, working three miles south of Canterbury, came across a buried Iron Age helmet. It looked initially just like the helmets worn in the First World War but when carefully handled by specialists it turned out to be a Roman helmet of the middle of the first century BC, exactly the years 55 to 54 when Caesar arrived. Technically it was described as a 'Coolas' type made of bronze in Gaul. Like latter-day Prussian helmets it had a spike for holding a plume, though this had been broken off. It could have been worn by one of Caesar's soldiers foraging across Kent, or perhaps been brought across the Channel by an itinerant salesman and purchased by one of the Kent soldiers resisting Caesar's conquering aspirations. One fascinating aspect of the helmet is that it had been used, up-side down, in lieu of a cheap, ceramic, funeral urn. The contents were the bones of a woman,maybe the wife of a widowed war-leader who wanted a prestigious grave for his beloved. The bones had been wrapped in a cloth bag fastened with a copper-alloy brooch. The spike, the brooch, and the helmet itself are displayed in Canterbury's Roman Museum.

In the period between Caesar's attempted conquest of Britain and the effective conquest by the emperor Claudius, rapid change took place and Kentish links with the continent intensified. Not only was the age-old practice of buying valuable, fashionable and elegant tableware enhanced, but social customs were borrowed and adapted from the expanding Roman republic-turned-empire. The kinglets of Albion minted their own coins in imitation of the coin-making traditions of Rome. Nobody in Canterbury would have worn woad, instead of cloth, as Caesar had claimed. Clothing, diet and politics had all become partially Romanised before the Claudian invasion. 'Celtic' kings, basking in the pretentious title of rex, visited Rome and came home with a Mediterranean glow of prestige and

This late Iron Age helmet, found near Canterbury in 2012, probably dates from Caesar's forays into Kent in 55 and 54 BC. © Canterbury Archaeological Trust Ltd

a taste for gambling and high living. The relationship has been compared to the relationship of the British Empire to the kings and princes of the twentieth-century Arab world who were educated in British public schools and trained at Sandhurst military college before returning home to rule their independent fiefdoms.

Trade between Britain and the Roman provinces, and especially imports of wine, continued to prosper after Caesar's attempted invasions but Colchester and Essex were more important markets than Canterbury and Kent. Since trade had flourished without the expense of an invasion it was not until the fifth decade AD that imperial rulers decided that conquest might be politically and economically advantageous. Politically the occasion arose when the emperor Caligula was assassinated in AD 41 and his low-profile uncle, Claudius, unexpectedly became emperor. Claudius was the fourth of the five god-emperors who were related in various adoptive and family ways to Julius Caesar and who between them governed the now formalised empire for its first hundred-odd years. To enhance his feeble status the new emperor planned a grand military enterprise of which his predecessors had sometimes dreamt. This was the conquest of the Ocean Sea, beyond Rome's Mediterranean world, a feat which had proved beyond the capability of the great Caesar himself. Even Caesar's famous heir, Augustus, had refrained from any attempt to conquer Britain, and although Caligula had built a lighthouse at Boulogne to facilitate cross-channel navigation he did not make progress in planning an invasion.

To plan his great enterprise Claudius sent his private secretary, Narcissus, to Boulogne. Narcissus was a highly educated former slave who rose through the ranks of the imperial bureaucracy to become the secretary-general of the Roman state. The secretary's instructions were to assemble 900 vessels, 5,000 cavalrymen, 10,000 pack-animals and 45,000 infantry. The invasion force was thus far larger than anything attempted by Caesar. It was, moreover, to carry its own supplies rather than attempt to live off the conquered land as Caesar had once done. When all the logistics were ready, and southern Britain had been 'pacified' by an initial invading force, a signal was to be relayed to Rome. The emperor would then sail to Marseille, cross Gaul, and follow up the invasion with a sixteen-day progress through conquered Albion. He would then return to Rome, a ten-week journey of 1200 miles, for a triumphal procession which would consolidate his hold on power. The huge-scale planning of the enterprise took two years. The legions chosen were the II, the IX, the XIV and the XX. The auxiliary forces from Germany and the Low Countries were promised that at the end of their service they would be allowed to marry, receive a tax holiday, obtain citizenship and settle in colonised Britain as gentlemen farmers

The invasion force was divided up into eight-man sections each with its own tent, mule, saw, axe, sickle, chain, rope, spade, baskets and satchels. Rations, skillets, pots, pans and clothing were carried in string bags. The mule trains carried corn, bacon, wine, beer, venison, fish, poultry and vegetables. The supplies were supplemented by barbecued foxes, voles, badgers and beavers as well as any sheep or oxen which could be lassoed along the road. Each centurion's set of eight-man sections had a two-wheel cart or occasionally a four-wheeled wagon. Some of the ships used to cross the Channel and enter the Thames were so large, fifty feet long and displacing 100 tons, that they could have carried elephants. Coins showing Claudius riding in style in a chariot drawn by no less than four elephants suggest that he could, perhaps, have made a regal progress in such a prestigious vehicle. Before calling on the emperor to come up from Rome, however, his commanding general, Aulus Plautius, had to make sure that any hostile indigenous peoples had been truly defeated and that the land was safe for an imperial victory parade. Since the men of the resistance knew the roads, the forests and the marshes, and could supplement their war-chariots with mounted cavalrymen, a Roman victory was not certain. Plautius did, however, have one important advantage which Caesar did not have. Some chiefs had lost their land in internecine wars in south-east Britain and had taken refuge among their countrymen in Gaul. These refugees were now happy to return to Britain with the Roman forces as path-finders, interpreters and spies in the hope of recovering their land, and perhaps even their status, under a new imperial regime. Plautius also had one wholly unexpected advantage. When his troops were assembled at Boulogne, fearsome rumours began to spread through the embarkation camps that supernatural forces governed the 'mysterious' island the invaders were expected to attack. The result was mutiny. When intelligence of this mutiny reached Kent the forces preparing for resistance were stood down. The men went home to harvest their crops. The Romans rapidly quelled the mutiny, re-mobilised the troops, and crossed the Channel without resistance. Some landed at Richborough, twelve miles from Canterbury, on a site which was to become a major industrial, commercial and military base for the next four hundred years. In AD 43 the colonising columns of soldiers, probably joined by others who had landed at other beaches, moved rapidly to cross the Medway and the Thames on their way to Colchester which became the most important garrison town in Britain and the place which Claudius entered to proclaim victory.

Canterbury did not become a garrison city like Colchester but a civilian one of some size, importance and comfort. The city was built on the Iron Age settlements next to the narrow river crossings. These old settlements, sometimes described as 'Belgic' (in heavy inverted commas) may have been settled by immigrants from the Continent, possibly refugees from the northward expansion of the Roman Empire. The arrival of the Roman legions led to the building of an improved highway from Richborough to Canterbury. Soon afterwards a grid plan of city streets was laid out on riverside land which now lies six feet below ground level. As early as AD 50 the streets were being flanked with buildings of timber and flint. As the soft ground was consolidated a more substantial building with masonry footings and a portico could be erected on the north side of the High Street. A basilica and a forum were built on the south side and some of the public buildings were enhanced with a veneer of marble. The importance of Canterbury as a religious centre where people from the surrounding clans met on neutral ground to honour the gods, was reinforced by the building new temples dedicated to the Roman gods, Diana, Juno, Venus, Ceres, Neptune, Mars, Jupiter and others.

Most country folk in the surrounding area carried on their Iron Age style of living in the early Roman years but some moved into the town and developed a whole new way of life. Rural households hitherto accustomed to subsistence living sometimes became city dwellers who earned wages paid in coin. Working for wages, measured in timed work-shifts, was a radical innovation for labourers accustomed to measuring their productivity in bales of hay or haunches of venison. The city provided a new market place for those who remained in the countryside. Woodsmen were able to sell quantities of building timber to townsmen. Out in the Blean forest demarcation boundaries between woodland plots were thrown up using Roman yardsticks. Roman earth mounds-and-ditches can still be traced, beneath the medieval boundary markers, by archaeologists using divining rods. On the grasslands shepherds found new cash buyers for both wool and mutton. Corn merchants supplied grain to millers who established water wheels on the streams, like those discovered at Ickham, a few miles outside Canterbury, and sold flour to the city bakeries. Some country-dwellers were co-opted into Roman society as all-purpose slaves to undertake such arduous work as chopping wood, stoking furnaces and stacking market stalls.

As Canterbury's economy developed, the coinage system became ever more important. Roman-type coins had been adopted long before the Claudian invasion but the quantities of coins in circulation increased dramatically after the conquest. One of Claudius' coins was stamped with the words 'De Britann' to celebrate his great feat. One extraordinary archaeological find relating to the Claudian invasion is a hoard of gold coins unearthed at Bredgar, on the road to the Medway. The latest of the thirty-four gold coins is dated AD 41, the first year of Claudius' reign. One might speculate that a paymaster in the Claudian invasion force had buried the money for safe keeping before challenging the British forces defending the Medway crossings. The value, weight and purity of Roman coins were in constant flux but a gold coin might have been worth eighteen silver ones and a silver one ten bronze or copper coins. The smallest coin, used for trading rather than for paying salaries and taxes, was called the *as* and came either as a whole coin or as half and quarter coins. Four of them made a *denarius,* a term corrupted as the *denier* of France or the penny of Britain, a coin which until the late twentieth century was still abbreviated by the letter 'd' rather than 'p'. When Canterbury was being extensively refurbished in the third century AD the old timber buildings of the St George's area were cleared away to make space for a masonry house with plastered walls and mosaic floors. It was here that one Roman had tried to hide his wealth and buried a hoard of no less than 700 coins.

One difficult question in the history of Canterbury concerns the magnitude of the population of Roman Kent. One speculation suggests that the future county was occupied by about 100,000 people, mainly Kent natives but with a significant minority of soldiers and settlers. As some half-dozen towns grew they may have drawn in as many as one fifth of the total district population. The smaller towns were Dover, Reculver, Lympne, Rochester and Richborough, but about half of the urban population probably lived in Canterbury itself. At its height in around AD 300 the city may have had as many as 9,000 residents. By then the city wall enclosed some 140 acres and the population, although smaller than that of Winchester or Cirencester, may nevertheless have amounted to about one third of London's population. Many residents would have been artisans, servants and slaves. A few city people might have been Roman soldiers or imperial mercenaries, but most of the military were probably quartered in the coastal towns. It has been (very speculatively) suggested that at the time Britain as a whole may have had a population of three million, but of these a mere 100,000 were Romanised soldiers and their extended families. As a long-settled part of Britain it is likely that the proportion of the Kent population under arms may have been quite small, perhaps only a couple of thousand members of army units, as compared to the larger detachments on the frontiers of north and west Britain.

A pictorial reconstruction of Canterbury in AD 300 can be seen in the basement of Waterstone's bookshop in St Margaret's Street. The largest Canterbury temple was probably located near the crossing where the High Street traversed the Stour River. There would have been other smaller temples in the town and private temples in domestic houses. The temple was next to the forum with its great portico of colonnaded arches. The Waterstone's picture also shows some of the high-status houses of brick with tiled roofs which existed in the city centre. One such house was built on riverside land which had been adequately drained and now lies underneath the twenty-first century Marlowe Theatre. The walls of this terraced house were painted in white, red, blue and yellow. Although many of the bricks and stones were later quarried out for the building of a nearby church and a friary, the waterlogged conditions meant that a wooden threshold, and even a builder's wooden spade, survived 2,000 years of airless immersion. Another important urban Canterbury dwelling occupied the site of the old Canterbury tannery between the two branches of the Stour at the western end of the city. This was an aisled domestic building, relatively large at thirty-odd Roman feet in width and perhaps two or three times as long. The complex was excessively difficult to excavate owing to the poisonous nature of the effluent which had been secreted by the tannery in recent centuries. The adjacent industrial branch of the river had probably been canalised in the third century to make the river deeper and narrower. This new cut may have had hard-standing quays since the river was still navigable up from the coast.

An insight into daily life in Roman Canterbury can best be gained by a leisurely visit to the Roman museum in Butchery Lane. Clothing was an important means of displaying status in society. The old tradition of sheep-rearing continued and woven textiles were carefully looked after. Roman crafts included embroidery and fine needles were made of bone. The Romans got though many pairs of leather sandals, or boots in cold weather. After clothing, cookery was an important and varied art. New types of fruit and vegetable were brought over from the continent by the colonisers – cherries, onions and herbs were all popular. Wealthy Romans imported some of their crockery from France and red shards of Samian ware are to be found on Canterbury sites. Even more expensive was the fine glass ware which the elite bought in the Roman city of Cologne in Germany.

The height of sophistication in a Roman household concerned art. Some fragments of wall plaster have been found in excavations in the St John's area of Canterbury but in Dover artistic material has survived in the form of whole mural paintings. Delicate floral decorations cover the walls of Dover's Painted House. In Canterbury a section of mosaic flooring can still be admired *in situ* in the museum basement. Tessalated floors with sophisticated mosaic portraits and geometric designs were regularly built into the floors of the Roman villas. Of equal interest, at the other end of the artistic scale, is a tiny engraved piece of Turkish gem-stone which fell out of a ring-setting two thousand years ago. The piece is only six millimetres high and it takes a magnifying glass to discern the figure of Cupid offering a

In about AD 300 Roman Canterbury, 'Durovernum', had fine brick and tile houses, hot and cold baths, a forum, a temple, and a huge terraced theatre. Drawn by John Atherton Bowen © Canterbury Archaeological Trust Ltd

Domestic Roman objects. All made of copper alloy. Group includes (clockwise from top) a brooch, nail cleaners, cosmetic or medical implement, tweezers, needle and spoon. Found at the Whitefriars excavations, Canterbury, Kent (THE BIG DIG). © Canterbury Archaeological Trust Ltd

dish before an altar. From the same site below the Beaney Museum a necklace, still with its closed clasp, has been found. It is of fine, elegant, workmanship and composed of figure-of-eight gold links. One could imagine that some Roman woman would have been sad to lose it below the floor boards of her house but the boards protected the necklace from heat when the house burnt down. Fire was a constant hazard in Canterbury since not all Roman houses were built of sturdy brick and many, even in the city centre, were timber-framed, just as they later were in medieval times.

One of the architectural problems faced by Romans, and indeed by all other generations of Canterbury architects, was the absence of any good-quality stone which could be cut and shaped for high-status buildings. There was also a complete absence of slate such as was used for roofing in the west of Britain. Wood and thatch had served the people well for nigh-on 8000 years but Romans decided to build in brick and tile. Clay pits were dug on both banks of the Stour and brick earth was excavated in the suburbs. Kilns which had long been used for firing pottery were now adapted to fire bricks and many kiln sites have been found. Such industrial sites stretched across the St Augustine's region on the south side of the city and in the St Dunstan's area on the north side. The almost revolutionary Roman brick industry served Canterbury's citizens well for a thousand years. Each successive wave of immigrants, Saxons from the north and Normans from the south, was pleased to find re-usable bricks taken from ruined Roman homes, theatres, temples, or bathhouses. Recycled bricks were employed to build walls, churches, forts and homes. Roman tiles, with their overlapping flanges sawn off, made particularly strong building material. Not until Tudor times did a new brick industry begin to flourish in Kent and eventually supply many of the 'stock bricks' needed to build London.

At the height of Canterbury's Roman prosperity wealthy citizens decided to replace their old theatre with a spectacular new one. The old theatre may have had earthen terraces banked up to face a stage but the new theatre was a much more elaborate affair and was built of bricks rising to three storeys. The stone kerb of the stage lies underneath the Three Tuns public house in Castle Street. On high days and holidays the great semi-circular terraces may have held as many as three thousand cheering, toga-clad, Romans or Romanised Britons. The performances were drama and music. Entertainment for the civilised citizens of Canterbury was probably rather different from that preferred by the garrisons on the coast or the working population of the countryside. Canterbury apparently had no amphitheatre for racing, with its associated gambling, though one such venue might have existed outside the city wall, underneath the police station on the Old Dover Road. The great brick theatre, designed to stage Greek tragedies and comedies, would have been unsuitable for war games or gladiatorial fights, though such human blood sports surely were performed in Britain as has been demonstrated by finds of mutilated bodies in York. Chariot-racing, the sport of emperors, also took hold in Britain as seen in the great arena at Colchester. One possible site of a Kentish amphitheatre is an unexcavated mound near the garrison town of Richborough.

The re-building of the Canterbury theatre was matched by an equally dramatic decision to enhance the civic importance of the city by building a mile-long wall all the way round the enlarged perimeter. The wall might have had some military justification. It could, perhaps, have kept immigrant peasants (who were beginning to cross the North Sea from the marsh lands of lower Saxony) out in the countryside rather than allowing them into town. It may also, like medieval walls, have been designed to protect the city from the night-time attention of brigands. But above all the wall was a statement of power and prestige. It was built at a time when Rome itself was building a great perimeter wall. Within the Canterbury walls eight gateways were cut, although most were not as magnificent as the medieval gateways which later replaced them. The Roman wall was, and in places still is, more than ten feet tall as can be seen next to the old Burgate. It was also more than five feet thick as can be seen in front of the Parrot Restaurant in St Radigan's. One piece of well-preserved wall built into St Mary's church in Northgate shows not only the flints, both whole and broken, but also larger stones brought from the coast. The London Gate, eight feet wide, has long disappeared from the field near Toddler's Cove but the shadow of a similar gate can be perceived in the wall on Broad Street not far from the postern gate into the cathedral precincts. Both the Roman gate and the postern gate have been called 'Quenin' or 'Queen's' Gate after the Merovingian princess from Paris who allegedly passed through on her way from a royal residence on the site of the future cathedral to the old temple on the hill which became the church of St Martin. The sheer outer wall on either side of the gate is faced with flint but the inner face of the wall was banked up with earth along the top of which sentinels could patrol. A small museum window showing one of the inner wall towers can be seen at the Canterbury bus station.

On the outskirts of Canterbury large areas were devoted to cemeteries. For a century or more Romanised citizens, like their British ancestors, preferred to cremate their dead. Cemeteries were filled with urns and pots containing the bones and ashes of the forebears. Cremated bones often survive better than unburnt ones in acid soils. The cremation urns were buried with an offered selection of flagons, beakers, cups, bowls and platters. Other graves contained mirrors, lamps, weapons and little statues. The ritual of cremation was probably also associated with animals and plants and perhaps the scattering of food such as beans and nuts on the pyre. One large cremation cemetery (marked on the Ordinance Survey map of Roman Canterbury) was located on the Old Dover Road 300 yards outside the city wall under the future site of St Sepulchre's nunnery. An even larger cemetery stretched beyond the river in the parish of St Dunstan, below the site of an eighteenth-century synagogue. Excavations carried out in 2011 revealed several hundred skeletons. Although poorly preserved their analysis may be able to tell us much about the Roman way of life and not merely about Roman funerary customs. A rather better preserved crema-tion graveyard of the second century was located at Durolevum, now called Ospringe near Faversham. Gradually, however, the custom of burying rather than cremating the corpses of the deceased became the Roman norm, Shoes, to be worn in the afterlife, seem to have been supplied to the deceased as votive offerings. Inhumation was later much favoured by Christians. They continued nevertheless to locate their cemeteries, and dig their new-style inhumation graves, beyond the city boundaries. Romans not only dug graves but also built ceremonial mounds over the top of them. One such mound on the city ring road had a car show-room perched on top of it. Another, the famous Dane John 'dungeon' mound, was originally outside the grid of residential Roman streets and must therefore predate the third century growth of the Roman city and the building of its wall. This mound was later greatly heightened and extended first by a Norman nobleman, Duke William 'the Conqueror', and later by an eighteenth-century tycoon, Alderman James Simmons. Other graveyards are to be found in what became the site of the eleventh-century Norman castle and the nineteenth-century railway station.

Much attention was given in Canterbury to the afterlife needs of deceased ancestors, but the well-being of the living also received extensive attention. Baths, like theatres and temples, were a central part of imperial life. The city of Pompeii had three great complexes of public baths. The city of Canterbury (a little smaller with perhaps 9,000 as opposed to 12,000 regular residents) had two known public bath houses. One of them lies six feet under the street between Waterstone's bookshop and the former church of St Margaret where Chaucer's Canterbury Tales are now re-enacted. This bath complex, adjacent to the great theatre, to the temple, and to the forum along the High Street, had seven rooms. The hot room, a sort of Turkish sauna called *caldarium,* had an unusual semi-circular apse. Beyond this apse lay the furnace which was stoked by slaves who coppiced and chopped enough wood in the great Blean Forest to keep hot air running through the ducts underneath the floor even in the bitter weather which was so alien to immigrants from Italy. The columns of tile which supported the *hypocaust* floor, a blackened chimney base and some signs of green bath algae, are still visible in the bookshop basement. Water for the hot bath was warmed in leaden tanks, also heated by hot air, and box-flue tiles carried the furnace fumes up though warm walls to vents at roof level. A tiled drain carried the polluted waste water out to the sewer. The whole complex stretched out under the future church to cold rooms, plunge pools and massage parlours. The baths may have had separate entrances for men and for women or, as elsewhere, women may have been able to use the baths in the mornings and men in the afternoons. The St Margaret's baths appear to have been upgraded and modernised about 300 AD.

A second complex of Canterbury baths was located a few hundred yards away, in the parish of St George, underneath W.H. Smiths. For some time this zone had been beyond the edge of the city and signs of agricultural ploughing were still visible into Roman times. This bathhouse, first built around AD 230, was on a relatively small site but had no less than twelve rooms including reception rooms, changing rooms, cold rooms, hot rooms and at least three separate baths. The whole complex survived in part by being sealed under a paved street which was frequently re-metalled in later centuries. The underfloor vents from the furnace to the hot room and hot baths were preserved intact. In AD 360 the complex was extensively renovated and the flues carrying the heat were tightly fastened together with iron clamps. The effluent from the baths was drained off into a deep soakaway. Since no filtering system was used the baths tended to became unhygienic if the water was not regularly changed and Roman soldiers with open wounds were advised against bathing lest their sores become infected. The source of fresh water for each change in the baths was from springs in the nearby Scotland Hills, later to be the home of a garrison of Argyle Highlanders. An excavated section of the Roman water channel shows the supply flowing through a duct six inches wide and six deep. This duct had a concrete lining and a sealed barrel vault of reused brick and tile. This water source was later chan-nelled into a pipe to supply fresh water to the medieval cathedral. Roman Canterbury had not only public baths but also private baths built into expensive town houses. One such civic residence with its own heated bathhouse was located on a site later known as the Longmarket. Out in the countryside agricultural estates of wealthy gentlemen-farmers also had private bath houses and one villa at Wingham, on the road to the coast, had a fine mosaic floor of which fragments have been found. Most Romans and Romano-Britons could not, of course, afford to build private bath houses and thus the public ones became the social focus of city life.

It has sometimes been assumed that Roman bath houses, like

ROMAN SOLDIERS AND SETTLERS

medieval ones, catered not only for hygiene but also for sexual appetites. Cohorts of young men of seventeen or eighteen arrived in Kent as soldiers full of adolescent testosterone. It seems likely that they may have sired broods of Romano-Celtic children, just as the British army in nineteenth-century India sired thousands, if not millions, of Anglo-Indian children. Marjorie Lyle's vivid piece of children's fiction describes how a young girl with blond hair gradually came to realise that her father was not her real father but that she was the daughter of a Nordic Roman mercenary. The fictional child witnessed the murder of the Romanised soldier who had raped her mother fifteen years earlier and she somberly took part in his burial, complete with his helmet and his sword, beneath the earthen floor of her hut. The question of sex in Roman Canterbury is one still shrouded in prudery. The tip of the iceberg was revealed, however, on a decorated piece of ceramic found under the basement of the Beaney Institute in the High Street. It shows a very proud figure obviously about to perform a very male act. Bathhouses, however, might not have provided the obvious venues for recreational sex. It is possible that the young women of Canterbury were not always the reluctant victims of male lust but on the contrary might have welcomed the embraces of prestigious conquerors. A significant section of the British population (which carried Roman culture, language and religion into the post imperial Romano-British age) were men and women whose fathers, though not their mothers, had been immigrants from every corner of the empire. The most successful soldiers and mercenaries were allowed to marry when they had completed their twenty five years of conscription. The wealthiest of them established large households in which they had ready access to the slave girls whom they purchased not only as serving maids but also as informal concubines. Second-generation slave girls were quite likely to be the daughters of the master and when being surreptitiously visited at night by the sons of the house could unwittingly have been engaging in incest. Such discrete activity was recorded on a Roman oil-lamp. Its inscription, loosely translated, says: 'I am a lamp, privy to the pleasures of your little bed: on it you can do what you like and I shall not say a word'. Many young bachelors, however, did not have access to their father's slave girls and so might have frequented rather sleazy brothels similar to a cramped five-berth one found under the ash at Pompeii.

In Roman times, as in later times, Canterbury was primarily a political and religious city. Beyond the civilian city walls, however, Kent was, and remained, important as a military staging ground right down to Napoleonic and even Churchillian times. Army barracks were regularly built and rebuilt. Although Britain only represented four per cent of the land surface of the Roman Empire it supported twelve per cent of the Roman army. The 50,000 men who held the province in subjugation were a huge drain on the exchequer and, as in all empires, the conquered people had to pay the cost of their own suppression. Many of these troops would have passed through Kent and the legions would have cast fear among their subjects. For military transit, Roman Canterbury was linked by four paved highways to four military and naval stations around the coast.

The port at Dover was built around 80 AD after the great rebellion led by Boudicca had been suppressed, but rapid and ready access to Britain still had to be available at all times. A well-paved highway was built which entered Canterbury by the great double-arched Riding Gate. It was expensive to maintain, the ditches had to be regularly cleared and the surface of rammed gravel had to be constantly up-graded. A more distant but very useful harbour was established at Port Lympne at the end of a road which left Canterbury by the Wincheap Gate and followed the Stour valley through the Downs. The closest naval station was at Reculver on the Thames estuary at the northern mouth of the Wantsum shipping lane. The barracks of a large garrison protecting the sea road to London stretched across half a dozen acres of a broad plain beside a black rocky promontory from which the Essex coast could be watched. A good Roman road linked Reculver to Watling Street, the great high road between Richborough and Canterbury.

Richborough was the most important of Canterbury's coastal towns. Coins pre-dating the Roman settlement indicate that its trading beaches had long been in use. The harbour had been a busy one for Iron Age shipping and remained a safe anchorage for Continental vessels using the Wantsum channel to reach the Thames. After the conquest the sea crossing was linked to a Roman commercial highway which came up through Gaul from Lyons, on the Rhone, to Boulogne. As trade increased, the Romans imposed taxes on their newly colonised subjects to finance the building of ever stronger walls around Richborough's maritime warehouses and industrial manufacturies. The most dramatic building in Roman Richborough was a great arch. It had four gateways facing in the four cardinal directions and was thought by some to be the largest ceremonial arch north of the Alps. On top of it was a fine golden statue which could be seen far out to sea, if not quite as far as the French shore. The Richborough arch was built on a high plinth, which still exists, and was coated in costly marble from Carrara in Italy. The work was eventually completed around AD 80 by the emperor Domitian to celebrate the final conquest of southern and eastern Britain by General Agricola. This arch eventually became the starting point for the great 'Antonine Way', a road which led right up to Scotland and was named after the son of the emperor Hadrian, the builder of the Scottish frontier wall. Over the next two centuries Richborough became both a military and a commercial city and its population probably rose to exceed that of Rochester in West Kent. As Richborough grew to thirty or more acres it built its own amphitheatre and a couple of temples. In the second half of the third century it also imitated Canterbury by building a huge curtain wall of flint and cut stone. Whether the wall was to protect merchants and artisans of the industrial hub from rural bandits or whether the wall (like the great arch) was a symbolic statement of pomp and prestige is not clear. It is even possible that the wall might have been built out of fear that sea robbers could cross from the Low Countries to plunder Roman trading harbours.

Watling Street, the great Roman highway from Dover to London, entered Canterbury by a monumental red gate, the Riding Gate. The wooden doors for its two carriageways swung on enormous hinges, one of which can be seen in Canterbury's Roman Museum. Drawn by John Atherton Bowen © Canterbury Archaeological Trust Ltd

In Roman colonies wealthy families, with extensive teams of retainers, established villas in country estates outside the towns. One such villa south of Canterbury was built at Folkestone early in the Roman period. It was located on a trading site which looked out across the Channel. The cliff top had long been an important industrial area for the making of agricultural grindstones from an outcrop of greensand rock below the levels of gault clay and white chalk. Folkestone made and exported hundreds (if not thousands) of greensand corn-grinding querns, and export models can be found all along the Kent coast and across the sea at Boulogne. Evidence for the importance of the trade is represented by finds of pre-Roman British coins, mostly of copper but some of silver and gold, and the trade increased in the hundred years separating the visits to Kent by Caesar and Claudius. When the Romans took control of Folkestone they very quickly built a villa on the site. The three-wing villa had a long outhouse containing a hypocaust and bathhouse which is now teetering on the very edge of the cliff above Folkestone's deep bay. The next cliff fall or earthquake is liable to tumble it into the sea. The oldest walls, with round-ended bays looking out to sea, were built of flint nodules and tufa, a soft limestone deposit which was quarried for the building of early Roman houses and later for medieval Kent churches. By AD 100 a new villa was built (this time of stone) with a square rather than a round frontage and with windows which may have had small glass panes or wooden shutters. Some of the large building tiles were stamped with a round 'CL.BR' imprint, Classis Britannicus, the imperial navy. This suggests that the villa may have been an official residence, or office, as it looked out across the Channel towards Boulogne where the Roman navy had its main base. The tiles may, on the other hand, have fallen off the back of an ox-cart and been quietly used for a local client by a cowboy builder. The villa could have been the house of an important Roman official who had retired to manage an import-export business within sight of the European mainland. Or it could have been the residence of a British household which had adopted Roman architectural styles and domestic manners over the years of contact with the Continent. It is also possible that the villa – and perhaps a surrounding agricultural estate – was the property of an upwardly mobile and heavily Romanised immigrant from a far-flung province of the empire who had served his time in the legions and gained the necessary licence, and the wealth, to establish a colonial family household with its complement of serving slaves. The status of the villa was demonstrated by a mosaic floor in the central hall. Following its discovery in the 1920s the mosaic was a visitor attraction until the outbreak of the Second World War when coastal sites were closed to the public. When the armed forces withdrew in 1945 the remnants of the mosaic were unfortunately collected as tourist souvenirs or became toys for local children. A wide-reaching community project (guided by professional archaeologists) is creating a detailed history of the site.

One of the best studied of the Roman villa estates lies thirty miles west of Canterbury at Lullingstone. The museum built over the site demonstrates the complexity of a Roman country house with its reception rooms, store houses, religious shrines, sleeping quarters and kitchen ranges. In the kitchen Romans enjoyed some culinary delicacies which might seem strange to a modern taste and others which remain familiar. They ate large snails fattened on milk and served with anchovy sauce. They stuffed their jugged hares with pine kernels and stoned dates and when hares were not available they ate dormice. Nuts such as Kentish filberts, walnuts and almonds were important as were savoury herbs such as dill, lovage, mint and garlic. Their range of vegetables included leeks, cabbages, lentils and cucumbers. One type of corn used to make bread was 'spelt' wheat. Grapes were the traditional Roman fruit but they also ate apples. Domestic livestock included milch cows, which were a little taller than those of the Iron Age, as well as geese and bees. Egg omelettes were eaten with honey. Wild game included pheasants, which may have been hunted with dogs, and river fish included eels. Cats were domestic companions whose paw marks were occasionally left on wet clay before it was fired.

By the late Roman period in the fourth century it is suspected that the owners of Lullingstone had discreetly adopted Christianity as their preferred religious practice. Evidence that the new faith had reached Kent before the imperial police force was withdrawn in AD 410 is to be found in the Roman museum at Canterbury where a cache of silver spoons with the Greek Chi-Rho symbol of Christ is on display. The spoons were dug up near the old London gate. The early Christian church excavated at Lullingstone was richly decorated with painted murals. The once subversive Chi Rho, the name

ROMAN SOLDIERS AND SETTLERS

of Christ, was boldly painted on the wall. The old Kentish and Roman gods were replaced by six life-sized priestly figures celebrating the life of Jesus of Nazareth. The closest parallels to these very early priestly images are to be found at the furthest end of the Roman Empire at Dura Europos on the Euphrates in Syria. The ante-chamber to the Lullingstone chapel was inscribed with the first and the last letters of the Greek alphabet, Alpha and Omega, signifying God in the Bible. No other Kentish farming estate has yet revealed signs of Christian worship but Christianity had become the official religion of the empire. Constantine had been persuaded that it was the god of the Christians, with the symbol of the cross on their shields, who had enabled him to overcome his enemies after his legions, based in York, had decided to support him in a bid for the imperial crown. This conversion took place around AD 313 and within forty years the owners of the Lullingstone villa had decided to adopt the new tradition. They may however, no doubt like many others, have hedged their bets by discreetly continuing to honour the old deities, to whom ritual urns have been found in the depths of their great house. Although the Lullingstone villa eventually succumbed to a fire which destroyed it, the memory of the Christian chapel may have resonated with the later Saxon and Norman settlers who built their own Christian chapels in the valley.

As Romano-Britons see sawed between honouring the old gods and worshipping a new one a small temple or shrine was constructed just outside Canterbury's eastern city wall, between the roads to Richborough and Dover. It was built around AD 340 when the new religion demanded that the old city temple be demolished. This small substitute temple was of a traditional octagonal shape. It may have had a wishing well into which the 260 coins which have been found could have been cast. Most of these coins are copper or bronze but a few are made of silver. They all date from the years 330 to 364 but came from mints scattered across the whole empire. Some may have been ex-voto thanks for services received and others promissory votive payments made in the expectation

The great industrial and commercial harbour at Richborough c. AD 300, as imagined from the air. © Historic England

of future divine help. Other objects unearthed include bracelets, pins, raspberry pips, pig bones and many other plant and animal remains. Libations may also have been poured from glass and ceramic vessels. A clue as to the shrine's purpose may be provided by fragments of a copper-alloy snake. The snake was the emblem of Mercury, the god of the travellers and businessmen who used

From the third century AD Richborough was surrounded by a twenty-foot wall with a flint core and cut stone facing. A similar prestigious wall was built around Canterbury c. AD 270.

Spoons from a silver hoard (c. AD 410) bearing the Greek chi-rho symbol reflect a Christian presence in late Roman Canterbury. © Canterbury Museums and Galleries

the adjacent high-roads. A shrine dedicated to Mercury might have been built at a time of revulsion against the new Christian religion and dismay at the closing of what might have been one of Britain's finer temples. This apparent reversion to 'pagan' worship did not last long, however, and the fine stone octagon and its ambulatory with possible glass windows was abandoned in the 360s as Christianity tightened its hold on Romanised society.

By the beginning of the fifth century change was afoot across the empire. Rome itself ceased to be the hub of empire it had once been and by AD 402 the seat of western government had removed to Ravenna in northern Italy. The eastern half of the empire was ruled from Constantinople on the furthest shore of Greece. In AD 406 a whole legion, the II Augusta stationed at Richborough, was withdrawn from Britain to serve in Gaul during a time of civil war. In 410 the emperor Honorius allegedly wrote to the British cities to say that they would now have to defend themselves against political turbulence without any imperial help. He claimed that he needed all his legions to protect his northern frontier against increasingly powerful Germanic nations such as the Goths and Vandals. Although the letter of 410 may be a misinterpretation of the documentary record, the drawing down of Roman troops in the early fifth century did happen. This led to a gradual changing of economic realities as army salaries ceased to guarantee money supplies. One last great deposit of coins, numbering about 20,000 pieces, was accumulated at Richborough shortly before 402. As the cash flow dried up important industries such as the potteries began to close down and the people of Britain reverted to using more home-made containers of wood or leather.

The decline of Roman influence, ideas and culture in Britain was relatively slow and the lights were not turned off overnight in the year 410. But the economic changes began to bite over the next generation. Coins were no longer minted and imports of such once essential commodities as wine dwindled. Once the army was no longer present, and being regularly paid, tradesmen suffered. As the administration began to fail the upper middle classes began to leave the impoverished city. In the countryside the magnates who owned villas had to become more self-reliant and became little warlords. Some of the Germanic mercenaries who had been a major part of the imperial presence may have stayed on. They might even have accepted the arrival of new Germanic immigrants, crossing the North Sea, even though the incomers would have been 'pagan' rather than Christian. As security declined new funeral fashions began to be adopted, burials took place nearer to home and the ire of the gods was allayed by the revived offering of sacrificial items on tombs. The decline of Roman custom was perhaps faster in Canterbury than in the west where Welsh kings, enjoying the affluence of their gold mines, and Cornishmen with their thriving tin mines, retained Roman traditions and links. But Canterbury did change and within a hundred years was facing up to a whole new set of cultural innovations coming no longer from the south but from the north.

PART THREE

SEA FOLK FROM THE NORTH

THE NORDIC peoples, who began to visit, raid and settle in Britain after, or even before, the withdrawal of the Roman legions came from all over northern Europe. It was the Angles who gave 'England' its new name, Angleterre in French, and the Saxons who amalgamated the native speakers into a single language entity which spoke Anglo-Saxon. Vikings came from as far away as Sweden and Russia, while Norsemen, later called Normans in French, came from Norway. One of the lesser-known Nordic groups were the 'Jutes' who settled in Kent and also on the Isle of Wight. The term 'Jute' is almost as controversial as the term 'Celt'. Some archaeologists are reluctant to differentiate 'Jutes' from other Scandinavian settlers but others continue to write of a distinctive 'Jutish' culture. Whence 'Jutes' came is not at all certain but the wet lowlands on the borders of Germany and Denmark seem to be a likely place from which they might have had to flee at a time of rising sea levels. Some 'Jutes' may have come from, or gone to settle in, 'Jutland' on the coast of northern Denmark. These 'Jutish' migrants were coastal seafarers rather than open sea ones like the Angles and Saxons who crossed the North

Sea to reach northern and eastern Britain. The 'Jutes' coming south would have seen the Isle of Thanet by the time they reached the southern beaches of Belgium. After crossing the narrow straits they beached their flat-bottomed, oar-driven, boats in the several creeks around the Wantsum channel. The evidence for the influence of these early migrating 'Jutes' is sparse and their age is known as the 'Dark Age'. This is not because the 'Jutes' were uncultured – far from it – but because they were slow to acquire the Roman art of writing. Much of their history is therefore based on such fragments as surviving place names and a growing accumulation of material artefacts which have been unearthed by archaeologists. By the time these Nordic immigrants began to arrive, the surviving era of the Roman cultural heritage was almost over.

One of the interesting questions about the development of Nordic culture in Kent concerns the role which might have been played by mercenary garrisons brought from Germany by Roman rulers to serve as the armed police force of the empire. Shortly before the Romans had to withdraw their forces from Britain – to cope with unrest in Gaul – a document made reference to a 'Saxon Count', perhaps a Roman official responsible for controlling the Kentish shore. Such 'Saxons', a people originally from the deep interior of Germany, may have been enemies threatening to invade or may have been legionaries who had been authorised to retire to estates around Canterbury after their years of service in the Roman garrison. A senior officer who married and settled in Kent might have adopted the title of count. The 'Saxon Count' may have been a serving Roman officer responsible for defending the British shore against 'Saxon' pirates, sea-beggars or invaders coming not from inland Saxony but from the lowlands of lower Saxony. Questions about the Nordic element in late imperial Britain and about the role of the 'Saxon Count' in Kent remain intriguing. Were 'Saxons' defending the Kentish coast or were they attacking it?

One of the ongoing mysteries of Canterbury history concerns the use of language. After the retreat of the Roman administration, the written word temporarily vanished. The spoken word changed, however, and for reasons which are by no means clear. On the European mainland, northern invaders adopted the language of their hosts and the 'Franks' who spilled into northern France learnt a Dark Age version of 'French' as did the later Norsemen who settled on the west coast of France. In Kent, by contrast, the immigrants brought their language with them and the local population began using 'Germanic' idioms. A similar change also occurred in eastern Britain where Nordic migrants (becoming perhaps fifteen per cent of the population) included women as well as men: the mother tongue of many locally-born children was thus a Germanic one. In Kent immigration may not have been as intense but was nonetheless influential. As old map names disappeared Durovernum, the Romanised 'Celtic' name of the city by the "river-all-set-about-with-alder-trees", became Cantwarabyrig, the stronghold or burgh of the men of Kent on the corner of the great island occupied by the Cantiaci. 'Jutes' may have given new names to other features of the landscape but it was not until a couple of centuries later that Saxon influence from northern Britain saw the return of writing when 'Old English' began to be used for charters concerned with land owner-ship and the administration of justice. Yet more change occurred when the Normans arrived in 1066 and brought 'Old French' with them as the language of the aristocracy. The common serving people continued to use an 'Anglo-Saxon' vocabulary but at the high tables in the halls of the nobility ox meat became *boeuf*/beef, swine chops became *porc*/pork and sheep's flesh became *mouton*/mutton. The change from 'Celtic' and Latin to Anglo-Saxon took place, however, during an age when literacy was in abeyance and clues as to the causes of change are scarce.

The arriving 'Jutes', unlike the Vikings four centuries later, did not find the Canterbury neighbourhood to be a rich one from which wealth in silver plate and coin could be extracted and carried away to a northern homeland. Instead they sought out land on which they could settle, preferably without too much disturbance to their long-established Romano-British neighbours. The city of Canterbury was itself partially abandoned during the fifth century and many Romanised former inhabitants congregated around old villa estates or created autonomous hamlets. The arriving 'Jutes' appreciated the fertile belt of Roman farmland which ran east and west, squeezed between the estuary marshlands of the Thames and the forested chalklands of the North Downs. As vacant land became scarce immigrants moved up the little valleys into the hills, clearing forest openings called 'dens' as they went. It is to be assumed that the 'Jutish' migrations were not military ones, consisting of male regiments like those of the Romans, but were composed of whole communities of men, women and children. They may have carried with them some of their more valuable livestock such as geese or even sheep. As they settled alongside the surviving Romano-British population they called the corner of Britain Kent and its people became the 'Kentings'.

Colonisers, both farmers and herdsmen, seeking new land were first attracted by the north-facing foothills of the Downs around Canterbury and later by a narrow strip of good farmland, with soils of mixed chalk and clay south of the Downs looking towards Folkestone. Population grew steadily until the Black Death, a thousand years later, and 'Jutish' colonisers had to intensify their land use both by penetrating the thick woodland and by exploiting a narrow belt of stony soils called 'chartland' bordering the great Wealden forest. Each geological layer in Kent ran from east to west and colonisation, spreading from north to south, exploited each soil opportunity in turn. The northern plain had the only trunk road in the region, Watling Street, but prehistoric drove ways and trade paths ran along the tops of the Downs. Nordic colonisers opened new 'hollow' ways up into the woods as they cleared 'assarts' for their crops. In the forest 'dens' they protected stands of oak and beech under which their pigs could be fattened on acorns and beechnuts. The seasonal 'drove-dens' for migrating livestock were at first only occupied in summer and autumn but over the centuries some became linked in small, permanent hamlets. The earliest year-round farms were established along the course of streams and rivers. The Little Stour, a few miles east of Canterbury, was known as the Bourne and ran through a particularly attractive valley. The industrial site of the old Roman water mills at Ickham became the centre of one 'Jutish' estate. Other stream-side communities took the name of the river: Great Bourne, now lost, Littlebourne, and later Bekesbourne, Patrixbourne and Bishopsbourne. When a new bridge was built across the stream for the road to Dover the surrounding village took the prosaic name of Bridge.

'Jutish' settlements along the Great Stour spread inland through the Canterbury marshes as far as Wye. The river, even if only minimally navigable, was a regular route through the hilly forest. One should, however, perhaps be careful not to associate the wildwood too closely with a great wilderness in which Hansel and Gretel could get lost. Only rarely did surviving wolves or angry boars kill children sent out to forage for birds' eggs and mushrooms. The serious problem in penetrating the Downlands was not impenetrable wildwood but the porous nature of the chalk soils. Spring water was scarce and thus restricted the land on which permanent farmsteads could rely on a year-round water supply for both people and cattle. In time the scattered 'Jutish' homesteads became loosely linked in a number of 'estates' focussed on places convenient for exchanging goods and news. In Kent the scattered pattern of small settlements was in marked contrast to the settlement pattern which Angle and Saxon immigrants brought to eastern 'England'. In East Anglia land was farmed in communal strips jointly managed with shared ploughs and oxen. Such cooperation was not a feature of the fragmented homesteads of Kent. In the open agricultural country of the Midlands husbandmen preferred to live in villages and went out to their fields at daybreak and only returned home at nightfall. In Kent, by contrast, farmers and pastoralists lived with their flocks and were closely surrounded by their fenced fields of crops which each household managed individually. 'Jutish' landowners travelled to periodic markets and fairs when they needed to visit an iron smithy or a cobbler's workshop. Crafts were primarily domestic and householders did their own carpentry, basket-making, spinning and tailoring without extensive resort to market exchanges.

Where new land (woodland and downland) was opened up, enclosures were defined and named in ways which survive to the present. Many place names refer to the maze of woods, lanes, fields, hamlets, streams, valleys, heaths, springs, ponds, marshes and commons recognised by the early post-Roman settlers. Between Canterbury and the south coast a thousand names of woods and coppices survive among the clearings that were carved out of the forests. The place names of these woods refer to the distinctive trees seen in them; oak, beech, birch, elm, hornbeam, alder, willow, yew, hazel, cherry, ash, holly, maple, crab-apple. One tree which is now ubiquitous, but which was allegedly not present until Norman times, was the sweet chestnut. Oak therefore remained the hard-wood of choice for both buildings and boats. Although Canterbury remained the cultivated part of Kent, which had been noted for its cereal crops and cattle herds by Caesar, it did have its own local woodland, the Blean forest. The poor soils of the Blean were never cleared for crops but only used for harvesting firewood or feeding pigs.

'Jutish' society was in sharp contrast to the bustle of Roman Canterbury with its crowded forum, its social baths, its market stalls, its status costumes and its leisure pursuits. The places where 'Jutes' did congregate were often small surviving remnants of the old estates surrounding Roman villas. As trade grew it generated a modest accumulation of wealth and wealth led to the search for power. Chiefs at the head of each 'Jutish estate' demanded food-tax in return for help with security against neighbours or brigands. The emerging markets attracted long-distance peddlers who sold imported wares which headmen could use to reward loyal tax-payers or sword-bearers. Payment for exotic luxuries from abroad could be made with woollen and leather goods woven and tanned by homestead artisans. Fine baskets were also made of willow and spliced hazel. 'Jutish' political estates became a distinctive feature of the countryside around Canterbury. In time the estates became the building blocks from which were constructed political 'lathes' used to administer Kent. Each lathe was measured in units of plough-land that a team of eight oxen could till in a year. Most of the half dozen 'Jutish' tribal lathes controlled not only fertile farmland and high woodland but also access to potential new grazing on the wetlands of the still poorly drained estuary marshes. The lathe which was responsible for Canterbury was based on the royal residence at Stour Gao, now Sturry, which administered the Stour valley from Godmersham down to the Wantsum waterway.

While the old Roman city of Canterbury was virtually neglected its wooden buildings fell into decay and its fine buildings crumbled

Coloured glass beads found in Sittingbourne in graves of wealthy Saxons.
© Canterbury Archaeological Trust Ltd.

This finely-worked early seventh-century gold pendant, unearthed in Canterbury, is in the form of a Byzantine Christian cross. It is now held in the city's Heritage Museum. © Canterbury Archaeological Trust Ltd.

into ruins which were later robbed out for brick, stone and tile that could be recycled when the city revived in a more prosperous 'Saxon' period. During the years of neglect the lower city silted up with leaf mould, moss, and river mud which formed a thick, black layer of soil quite unlike the red brick-earth on which Roman and Iron Age settlements had been built. The 'Jutes' had only a limited interest in reviving the city and built their royal residences on river estuaries as they did at Sturry on the bank of the Stour estuary. The pioneers who penetrated south from there may have by-passed Canterbury as they followed the various channels weaving though the Stour marshes. These pioneers preferred to live on their land, not in villages let alone towns.

By the sixth century Germanic ideas of statecraft began to inspire the people of Kent as the 'Jutes' established the first 'kingdom' in Britain. Since Christianity had lapsed with the decline of Rome, the new 'kings' sought legitimacy in legend. Their claimed ancestors were not the children of wolves, like Romulus and Remus in Rome, but rather of Hengist, the stallion, and Horsa, his equine mare. These military allusions to cavalry prowess were later taken by Saxon writers such as the Venerable Bede to refer to real persons rather than to symbolic claims to armed authority. The new idea of kingship required the accumulation of wealth. The Canterbury valley yielded adequate food crops and livestock to feed the local populations but was not rich enough to support royal patterns of consumption all year round. Kentish kings therefore maintained a network of royal villas in the country's more important districts and were constantly on the move visiting each estate in rotation. The city of Canterbury, still ringed by a derelict flint wall, was not one of these royal villas although it was regularly visited by kings. One important royal residence lay at Eastry. It was on flat land and much larger than the other lathes and had access to the east coast, ten miles from Canterbury, on a creek leading up from the lower Stour. Ten miles to the west of Canterbury, at Milton Regis, the 'Jutish' *villa regalis* acquired a royal name and retained especial privileges. Another royal estate was far to the south of Canterbury at Lyminge where it had connections with the south coast.

Lyminge is the most extensive 'Saxon-type' site near Canterbury, comparable in importance to Yevering in Northumbria. In the fifth century AD the site had been occupied by 'Germanic' settlers, possible calling themselves 'Jutes'. Their houses had traditional two-foot-deep sunken foundations and stout, timber, corner posts. In the seventh century a royal community built, and re-built, a series of great feasting halls. The first one was six metres wide with great, swung doors on both flanks, the second was wider still, and the third was a massive building with a span of ten metres. The roof was not supported by internal pillars but rather anchored to strong, angled, timber buttresses on the side aisles. The floors were cobbled with flint-and-mortar and with recycled Roman brick. The great timber walls would have sheltered up to a hundred guests. A chance find of the remnants of a sturgeon suggest that royalty in the 'vill' ate well off fish. Lesser folk ate limpets and oyster from the sea-shore. One midden contained the skeleton of a small horse, and another the heavy iron coulter of a plough. Fragments of slag, and of furnaces, suggest that occupants not only forged iron but also smelted it. All around grave goods tell of great wealth. Gold, garnets and silver were buried and coloured glass beads seem to have been relatively abundant. The site even turned up scales for weighing gold coin.

The post-Roman people of Kent may not have worn costly togas, but they did treasure personal ornaments. The most notable were brooches, used to fasten shawls or smocks and pinafores. Many every-day iron safety pins rusted away but costly ones were made of gold and were sometimes even enhanced with semi-precious stones cut and clasped by jewellers. One of the creekside landing places favoured by settlers was Faversham and it became an important centre of fine metal working. The industry started on a small scale under 'Scandinavian' influence but when 'Saxon' culture spread into Kent fine metalwork blossomed. The craft tradition lived on and the town's name derives from the Latin word *faber* or *faver* for smelting or smithing, as in French *orfèvre* meaning goldsmith. The town also seems to have developed an industry making vessels of blue glass. Trade at Faversham required skilled pilots to bring ships up to the several quays which handled heavy cargoes such as quern stones for the grain mills of a marshy and chalky farmland which had no stone of its own. Under Saxon rule the town became a prototype 'cinque port' which offered the king naval mariners in exchange for customs privileges. The mouth of the creek faced the Isle of Harty which, legend has it, featured in the classic adventures of Beowulf written in the dawn years of Anglo-Saxon literature.

Faversham jewellery, and other rare objects provide the main clues to 'Jutish' material culture, are found at burial sites. 'Jutes' did not regularly practise cremation but usually preferred inhumation. For their burial grounds they seem to have chosen places which inspired historic awe. The great barrow at Ringlemere, for instance, was close to the important royal estate at Eastry and was regularly re-used for pre-Christian burials. Such burials were enhanced with valuable grave goods, in particular jewelled brooches of a style also found in Denmark. The forty-odd Ringlemere burials of the fifth century also contain beads, rings, pins, buckles and some glass vessels. By the sixth century, when the Franks had established their rule over the mainland opposite Kent, high status graves were furnished with brooches and belt buckles of Frankish design. The finest objects included work with silver inlay, ornaments with bird designs, discs decorated with garnets and even headbands of gold braid. Bertha, daughter of Charibert of Paris and wife of Ethelbert of Kent, was probably not the only Frankish bride to be sent to Kent wearing a gold-braided headdress. Other valuable objects included beads of coloured Rhineland glass or of amber from the Baltic Sea. Kent, unlike Essex, has not yet yielded up golden heirlooms of Scandinavian design like those of Sutton Hoo but mundane tools of a Scandinavian pattern, including 'weaving swords' used to make woollen cloth, are found in graves along the Wantsum channel. New archaeological techniques can now find traces of the goods made of textiles. Woollen Kentish material, demonstrating gift exchanges or trade, has been found in Frankish graves across the Channel in Picardy. Hides and furs were also exported even though the population of bears and beavers was in decline. In the absence of mines, other than iron mines which 'Jutes' unlike Romans seem to have neglected, Kent made the most of what resources it had. One must assume that the cross-channel trade continued to feature slaves, probably including child slaves who were easier to capture and control than adults. Female children would have been particularly prized in a world of high mortality where the breeding of each new generation was important. It was probably export slaves who were used to pay for some of the costlier exotic jewellery found in graves.

Two major Nordic graveyards have been excavated within fifteen miles of Canterbury, one at Dover and the other at Sittingbourne. The Buckland cemetery at Dover contained at least 244 known tombs. It seems to have been used between AD 475 and AD 625. Some of the grave goods are military ones: spears, shields, swords, slings and an iron axe-head which could be a tool or a weapon. The huge range of domestic implements, including iron knives, wooden buckets, weights and scales, glass bowls, spindle whorls, tweezers and even lock keys, make it one of the largest post-Roman cemeteries to be discovered in South Britain. The jewellery finds were also spectacular, with garnets set in gold, amethyst bracelets, fine finger-rings, and disc brooches of Frankish design. A second major graveyard, 'The Meads' at Sittingbourne, has more than 200 surviving graves and is close to the great royal complex of Milton Regis. A few of the graves contained cremated bones in burial pots but the majority were unburnt burials in which occasional teeth were found but bone rarely survived. The haul of grave goods, however, was rich and one grave contained no fewer than 300 glass beads. Some of the graves were clearly designed for members of the elite. By AD 540 the nearby workshops of Faversham were in production and one grave contained a blue glass beaker. One feature of the Sittingbourne graveyard was that three-quarters of the graves contained weapons of war, notably shields. The culture of the graveyard owners was 'Nordic' though there is little evidence of Scandinavian artefacts as opposed to Frankish ones. Grave goods apparently came by trade links rather than as the property of migrants. The choice of site for the graveyard was, as at Ringlemere, one with old ritual significance dating back to the Bronze Age or before. Its use during the time when 'Jutish' culture was percolating into Kent culminated around the end of the seventh century.

One of the finest known pieces of early Kent jewellery was found in a graveyard in a western suburb of Canterbury where the Romans had once developed a huge cemetery. The piece is a 'pendant', a form of jewellery which supplemented the ornate brooches which held a woman's clothing in place. Some pendants had representations of Nordic gods such as Woden and others depicted animals. The Canterbury one was a circular pendant suspended by a barrel-shaped loop. It was made of gold, decorated with filigree wires, and held inlaid 'cloisonné' garnets backed with gold leaf. It was crafted in the seventh century, possibly as early as AD 620. The style was a local adaptation of Byzantine jewellery fashion and included a Christian cross of the Eastern Roman empire. Signs of wear show that it was well used during the lifetime of its owner. Although there is no evidence of an associated burial it may have been pinned to a noble lady of the royal court for her funeral on a site of ancient ritual importance. The pendant is now displayed in the Canterbury Heritage Museum.

In the city of Canterbury itself evidence for spasmodic occupation after the decline of Rome is somewhat sparse. People who had adopted the Nordic lifestyle of the fifth and sixth centuries did build small wooden houses within the crumbling city walls and some of these houses had sunken floors dug into the black earth which had accumulated over the ruins. One such building, in what later became the parish of St George, contained carbonised grains of cereal suggesting it might have been a granary which burnt down. There are signs of industrial activity inside the walls and under the old Roman gate arches on Watling Street. Successful city traders prized beautiful objects such as an ornate fine-toothed comb. Post-Roman trade appears to have been largely undertaken by the exchange of goods during the temporary absence of coinage. Weaving remained an important industry, with loom weights gradually gaining in size as looms became larger. The dying of hanks of wool with red madder, a craft which had attracted early Roman merchants seeking Kentish textiles, continued to be practised. Ceramic industries, on the other hand, declined and the common folk ceased to use pottery wheels for throwing pots and reverted to using hand-made pottery tempered with grass rather than crushed minerals.

Two centuries after the decline of the traditional Roman Empire a new Roman 'empire' began to take root in Kent. This one was based not on military power but on religious influence. Canterbury became the headquarters of a Romanised church headed by a pope who normally resided in the old imperial city. The Roman church gradually acquired the name 'catholic' and claimed a universal outreach. In time it won supremacy in Britain and eclipsed the old Christian traditions of the 'Celts' which had survived the fall of old Rome in the western and northern regions of the British Isles. In Canterbury the old imperial Christianity had died out before AD 600. Romano-British religious culture had largely been replaced by Nordic cultures spreading down from the Germanic lands. This new religion was neither Roman nor Christian and its gods were the ones which Britons adopted in place of the Roman gods for their days of the week. Mercury's day, preserved in France as *mercredi,* became Woden's day, Wednesday. Saturn, however, survived as the Saturday god.

From about AD 600, at the end of the second century after the departure of the Roman legions and the arrival of the 'Jutish' farmers, literacy began to return to Kent and in the fullness of time oral history began to be picked up and passed to chroniclers such as Bede. This documented history of Canterbury has, unsurprisingly, tended to focus on the religious history of the city. Religious history relates to the close contact which Canterbury retained with the nearby mainland. The cultural, economic and political influence of the Frankish kingdom of northern France brought in its wake a new version of Christianity. The relationship between Christianity and the art of writing meant that the surviving chronicles give undue prominence to the reign of King Ethelbert who reigned from about AD 560 until his death about AD 616. Ethelbert, who claimed descent from the great god Woden, was the most senior of the kings in Britain. As 'the first among equals', he may have settled political disputes as far north as the Wash or even the Humber.

Ethelbert's status was such that the powerful Merovingian dynasty of the Frankish kings in Paris considered it advantageous to send one of the king's daughters, the Christian princess Bertha, to Kent as a trophy bride and as a diplomatic envoy to Ethelbert's court. To cement the Paris connection Ethelbert gave his bride, and her chaplain Liudhard, a residence inside the old city wall of Canterbury. It was she, legend says, who went out through the 'Queningate' to

By late Saxon times Canterbury's cathedral was thought to have two octagonal towers, an apse at the west end, and a cloister for its community of monks. Drawn by Ivan Lapper © Canterbury Archaeological Trust Ltd.

maintain the French custom of daily Christian worship in the disused Roman temple on the hillside overlooking Canterbury. This 'chapel' was named after the patron saint of France, St Martin, the holy man of Tours who had shared his cloak with a beggar. According to Bede's history of the English church, Bertha's household met there to sing the psalms, to pray, to say mass, to preach and to baptise.

The prestige of the Merovingian dynasty to which Bertha belonged was ubiquitous in the royal villas of Kent. Ethelbert, who may himself have had some Frankish ancestry, was anxious to establish his autonomous kingly status and not become a Merovingian pawn tied to his wife's apron strings. He wanted to be seen as a major figure on the European scene rather than as a mere off-shore

Ethelbert, the 'Jutish' king of Kent, married Bertha, a Frankish Christian princess.

princeling. The road to status seemed to lie through the adoption of Christianity. But Ethelbert was not content to be converted and baptised by an honorary bishop sent over from France as a chaplain. He wanted to be converted by a proper bishop sent by the pope himself. And so it was that Pope Gregory arranged for a major mission to be sent to Canterbury. Gregory's political motives were probably not those of legend. This legend, recovered by Bede, claimed that the pope had been shocked to see fair-haired 'Angle' children from 'England', looking like angels, on sale in the regular Roman slave market and decided that the 'English' should be converted to Christianity. In real politics he was more concerned to spread his 'catholic' empire across the sea to the British Isles, consolidating his

hold on France in the process. Indeed he may have been visiting the slave market looking for young British boys who could be trained to support his mission enterprise. The mission he eventually sent consisted of forty men, four of them monks, led by an elderly and rather reluctant priest called Augustine. Within a year of its arrival Augustine's mission had converted and baptised King Ethelbert and made Canterbury the headquarters of an 'English' church.

Relations between church and state did not initially run smoothly in Kent any more than they had done in France. Bertha's father had at one point been excommunicated by the pope and therefore gave some of his inheritance to the children of his concubines rather than to those of a Christian wife. In Canterbury Bertha's son Eadbald also

This ornately decorated knife dates from the time of the Viking raids on Canterbury.
© Canterbury Museums and Galleries

gave up the church. It may have seemed to him that to abandon the protection of the old Norse gods was just too risky. What is more the new king dismayed the church when he attempted to secure the family network of power by marrying his widowed step-mother, a Frankish princess who had married Ethelbert after the death of Bertha. The hiatus in church affairs caused some upheaval and the two dependent bishoprics which Canterbury had created in Rochester and in London thought it prudent to send their bishops home to France during the revival of Nordic religious practice. The new king's religious lapse, making sacrifices to the pagan gods in the woods, was relatively short-lived. Like his father, he accepted public baptism and incorporation into the world of Christian French culture rather than pagan Nordic culture. In Canterbury the new church traditions rapidly took hold and spread Christianity once more across Kentish society.

When Augustine had arrived in Canterbury the city saw a burst of building activity after two centuries of decay. The momentous arrival of the great mission created the need for a suitable permanent home. The abbey which Augustine proposed to build was to be situated outside the city wall. The abbey church would then serve not only for worship but also for the entombment of kings and bishops. The old imperial tradition of Rome had been to build tombs outside the city wall and this tradition was retained by the Augustinian mission. The church of St Peter and St Paul, named after the founders of Christianity, was built a few hundred yards beyond the north-eastern city gate on a site now called St Augustine's. Since new building material was, as ever, scarce in Canterbury the monks got their workmen to demolish half-ruined old Roman buildings and use the bricks and tiles to build their new church. In addition to the robbed and recycled material the builders also dug deep quarries alongside the road from Dover out of which they extracted heavy flints and also chalk which could be used to make lime mortar. Some of their 'ashlar' building blocks were cut from chalk although chalk was a friable material which did not stand up well to weathering unless the core of the wall was coated with a finish of cut flint and mortar. Over the centuries, as the abbey buildings were built and rebuilt to suit the changing needs and styles of the times, St Augustine's Abbey used no fewer than eighteen different types of stone brought in from elsewhere. Some of this stone material was hauled up the Stour on barges from the sea cliffs of Reculver.

The initial abbey complex consisted of three buildings. The westernmost was the church of St Peter and St Paul and it was here that, with a certain amount of shuffling of tombs, the graves of the first half dozen archbishops of Canterbury were placed. They were located in the northern chapel, off the main aisle. The southern chapel was reserved for kings and queens, especially Ethelbert and Bertha, but also for their original chaplain Liudhard. The side chapels, technically known as 'porticos', showed the cultural influence emanating at the time from Ravenna, one of the Byzantine jewels of northern Italy. A second, smaller, church was devoted to the Virgin Mary but little remained of it when a later archbishop decided to use the site for a dramatically new octagonal chapel at the east end of the abbey church. This octagon was never completed, however, and when the Normans arrived it too was demolished to make way for a new, larger and longer monastic church. The third of the three seventh-century churches designed for the new monks was dedicated to St Pancras, the patron saint of children. The western arch of the St Pancras building was later reconstructed and still stands unlike any other seventh-century building. This front arch was decorated with recycled Roman brick on a building which was otherwise largely made of flints from the river bed and the chalk mines.

Once Augustine was established in Canterbury, Pope Gregory mobilised reinforcements from Rome and a second team of missionaries arrived in AD 601. They brought with them a fine collection of vestments, to show off the importance of the church leaders, and illuminated books, to emphasise the scholarship of a church whose worship was rooted in literary texts. One sixth-century gospel has partially survived and in the twenty-first century is still used at the enthronement ceremony of archbishops. The second mission also brought beautiful silver plates and cups for the serving of the ritual bread-and-wine of the last supper, and even some quasi-magical 'relics' associated with the saints of old if not with Jesus himself. The original role of Bertha's Frankish chaplain in re-introducing Christianity to Canterbury was celebrated by the coining of a gold medallion with his name stamped into it, a medallion now held by Liverpool museum. The status of Augustine himself was enhanced by the granting of a papal 'pallium', an embroidered collar which gave him the rank of a 'metropolitan' bishop.

The building and rebuilding of the great complex of St Augustine's Abbey was matched by another huge construction project in Canterbury. This was the building of a cathedral inside the core walls of the old Roman city. Although Canterbury had not been one of the royal residences of the Kentish kings whose primary seats had been at Eastry and Lyminge and Milton, the city was nonetheless a place which inspired awe and was thus chosen for the building of a cathedral. The cathedral was not aligned with the Roman street grid but was built on top of the layer of dark earth which represented the years of decay. In style and size the first cathedral resembled the monastic church of St Peter and St Paul. It was about eighty feet long and thirty feet wide and was probably built within the life time of Augustine himself. About 150 years later, when burial customs were changing and burial outside the city wall was no longer deemed *de rigeur*, an extension chapel was built at the east end of the cathedral for the burial of archbishops. The change of tradition provoked severe conflict between the monastery and the cathedral as the prestige of having the right to bury archbishops carried great financial benefits through the offerings of pilgrims who visited the tombs.

When the religious hiccup which followed the death of Ethelbert had subsided Bishop Lawrence of Rochester and Bishop Mellitus of London returned from their exile in France. Each in turn was appointed to the seat of St Augustine. Their graves of AD 619 and AD 624 can still be visited in the ruins of the abbey although those of Bertha and Ethelbert disappeared during the Norman reconstruction of the church. Before the Norman Conquest thirty-odd 'metropolitan bishops', later referred to as archbishops, were enthroned in Canterbury. They presided over the English church during the four centuries preceding the Norman Conquest. Two of the archbishops, one a Greek from Asia Minor and the other a Saxon from the west of England, were noted reformers of the English church. Theodore of Tarsus, an elderly monk like Augustine, took on the administrative role but was particularly noted as a scholar. His study of religious texts used the original Greek and other eastern languages rather than depending on Latin adaptations. He, and his assistant Hadrian, set up a famous school, the first modern school in England, in Augustine's monastery. Monks were trained in scripture, poetry, astronomy, law, calligraphy and music. The music was probably plainsong and may have been named Gregorian chant after Gregory the Great who had sponsored the re-founding of the church in England. The discipline of the monks was tightened according to monastic 'rules' and in time the abbey became an autonomous Benedictine house and followed the Rule of Benedict. By the time of his death in AD 690 Theodore had unified the church in England

and established a lasting pattern of regional bishoprics. The status of Canterbury had also been enhanced after AD 664 when a synod held at Whitby determined that Canterbury's decision to adopt the Roman liturgical calendar, rather than the 'Celtic' calendar used in Ireland and Scotland, would set the agreed date of Easter.

The second of the great archbishops of Canterbury was Dunstan. He had been the Saxon abbot of the extremely wealthy abbey of Glastonbury in Wessex. Like Thomas Becket, in a later age, he was an appointee of the crown and had been *de facto* first minister of Wessex before, at the ripe age of fifty, becoming archbishop in AD 960. His career also paralleled that of Becket in that he became an informal saint soon after his death and for nearly two centuries his shrine was the most popular pilgrimage destination in Britain. Dunstan was the patron saint of goldsmiths which gave his name particular lustre. In popular folklore he was also famed for having tweaked the devil's nose with a blacksmith's tongs, an event depicted in church statues and recorded in the ditty:

> St Dunstan, as the story goes,
> Once pulled the devil by the nose
> With red-hot tongs which made him roar,
> That was heard three miles or more

Dunstan, like Theodore, was keen on monastic discipline and reformed the behaviour of Canterbury's monks. The monastery built by Augustine and dedicated to St Peter and St Paul was now re-dedicated and St Augustine's became the common name of the institution. By this time a community of canons had grown up beside the cathedral and Dunstan insisted that these canons, like the monks, should adopt the Rule of Benedict with a simplified lifestyle, personal poverty, obedience to the prior, and the recitation of the daily and nightly offices. Dunstan was especially noted as a calligrapher and draftsman of illuminated texts. He retired as archbishop in AD 978 but remained in Canterbury as a teacher until his death ten years later.

In the tenth or eleventh century the old cathedral was deemed too small for the enhanced status of its archbishops. It was cleared away so that the sanctified space could be used for a new 'Saxon' cathedral to replace the old 'Frankish' one. The new cathedral was twice as long as the old one, one hundred and fifty or more feet from its rounded western apse to its eastern altar. Two hexagonal stair turrets led up to the western apse and the altar may have been flanked by towers. The nave stretched all the way from inside the current west door to the edge of what became the great eleventh-century Norman crypt and choir. This rebuilt 'Saxon' cathedral may have had a tower, but if so a much stumpier one than the fifteenth-century tower known as Bell Harry. As the cathedral developed its own monastic priory on the north side of the precincts its scriptorium became famous for the preparation of illuminated texts. After the Norman Conquest, Christ Church Priory surpassed St Augustine's in terms of scholarship and manuscript crafting.

In the countryside around Canterbury, monks created 'minsters', some of which were given wealthy tracts of land by political rulers. One of the great minsters with Canterbury links was at Minster-in-Sheppey, where the island of sheep rose on high ground above the Thames marshes. The old Roman fort at Reculver also became a minster church. Its later western towers still stand and have long been a beacon to guide shipping entering the Thames. Some minsters acquired trading privileges. The powerful abbess of Minster-in-Thanet, for instance, was given a remission on the tolls that her sailors might otherwise have had to pay when trading up the Thames to London. She also had privileged landing rights in the creek at Faversham. Another important minster, with a noble abbess, was established on the royal estate at Lyminge. This was a 'mixed house' which had both male and female chapters. The original abbess, Ethelburgha, might conceivably have been the daughter of Ethelbert, and therefore the widow of a Northumbrian king, but the name was not an uncommon one and the association with Ethelbert is far from certain, though widely believed in folklore.

In the eighth century, when Lyminge seemed threatened by piracy in the English Channel, the minster was given a new home within the walls of Canterbury. The western corner of the city, formerly a Roman dwelling and later known for its great tannery, became a nunnery garden laid out with horticultural plots linked by walkways of brushwood across the marshy ground.

Once the church had restored literacy to Canterbury it was possible for legal custom to be codified. Early medieval law was as much about relations between people as about the ownership of property, even landed property. The law codes of Ethelbert and his heirs shed much light on the preoccupations of Ethelbert's people. Stealing was a great problem and stealing from the newly established church was an especial problem. Penalties rose with status and stealing from a mere clerk was punished less severely than stealing from a deacon or a priest or worse still from a bishop. Murder was also deemed to be a crime though not always such a serious one as theft. Fines for homicide ranged from six to fifty shillings. A more severe penalty was imposed on a man who dared to have carnal knowledge of one of the king's maidens, though if the maiden were a slave-girl his fine would be halved. Lesser penalties were spelled out for the sexual abuse of serving maids in noble rather than royal households and if the raped girl were the slave of a commoner the penalty was quite small. The buying and selling of maidens was also controlled by law. One item of the criminal code said 'if a freeman lies with the wife of another freeman he shall … procure a second wife with his own money and bring her to the other man's home'. Such were the prime preoccupations of seventh-century customary law. The question of quarrelling with weapons, or of lending a weapon to a highwayman, had to be assessed with a suitable scale of tariffs. If the victim of a highway robbery were a slave, the fine would be a mere three shillings. More complex tariffs applied to freemen even if they were merely bruised. Cutting a freeman to the bone cost three shillings, breaking a bone four shillings, and the loss of an ear six. Wounding the skull was fined at ten shillings but the loss of an eye was dealt with much more severely. Altogether injuries to thirty or forty individual parts of the body were listed, especially those to the 'generative organ'.

One hundred years after Ethelbert's reign the customary laws of Kent had some different priorities. The church had become so important that it was exempt from taxation but church members were required to pray for the king. A priest who was too drunk to perform his duties was to be suspended from office and a servant caught riding on horseback on a holy day was to be flogged. Making offerings to the devil was obviously a threat to society but it was not only slaves who were fined for so doing but also freemen. Feeding meat to one's servants on a fast day was also subject to penalty. Although witnesses in court were required to tell the truth under oath, kings and bishops were exempt from oath taking. When it came to property, the rights of widows and children were to be cared for, if necessary by a guardian until the child was ten years old. In matters of theft, the king could decide whether a criminal should be put to death or sold overseas. Strangers were seen as a constant threat and had to announce their presence on the highway by blowing a horn lest they be assumed to be robbers and could thus be summarily slain.

One of the changes which Ethelbert brought to Canterbury in the sixth century was a return of the use of currency coins. Some coins were far too valuable for every day transactions and were a store of wealth which could be hoarded. The golden *tremiss*, for instance, was a coin of twenty grams which was regularly cut up into smaller pieces for use by goldsmiths. Smaller silver coins were called *sceattas* and were widely minted in Friesland and Denmark, continental regions historically associated with the kingdom in Kent. By 630 these proto-pennies, each weighing not much more than a gram, were being made locally. The minting of coin was not the sole right of kings but was also practised under licence in abbeys and monasteries. It was said that by the ninth century, as coinage became current in both long-distance and local transactions, no less than seven mints were in operation in Canterbury.

In the two or three generations after the death of Ethelbert the wealth of the city of Canterbury revived but the political importance of the kingdom began to decline. The great Anglian and Saxon and Danish kingdoms of Mercia and Wessex and Northumbria rose to overshadow Kent. The distinctive 'Jutish' nature of Kentish social culture was gradually absorbed into the wider Germanic traditions of Britain to become 'Saxon'. Once again there was little sign of the movement of people but cultural, political and economic traditions changed. Kentish kings, who had once had great influence on the merchant traffic along the Thames, now lost their royal market hall in London. Mercian power stretched south from the Midlands to the Thames and beyond. The north coast of Kent was no longer secure when the East Saxons of Essex threatened the shoreline at Reculver. The change in politics related in part to changing attitudes to land as well as to changes in the control of trade. The exploitation of much of the land, perhaps a quarter of the whole kingdom of Kent, was in the hands of the minsters and abbeys. In an age of rising population the political control of land became increasingly important. Kingdoms became units of territory rather than primarily associations of kinship groups. Small personal regiments, led by aristocrats, now fought over parcels of land that were becoming more valuable. Noblemen who controlled such land sought the protection of kings who could muster armies to support their claims. By comparison with the rival Anglo-Saxon kingdoms, Kent was a rather small polity, and had become a weak one by the eighth century.

In the late eighth century, Offa of Mercia, who had defended the back of his Midland kingdom against the Welsh by building his great dyke, gained suzerainty over Canterbury and ended the independence of the 'Jutish' kingdom of Kent. Offa wanted closer commercial ties with his mainland contemporary, Charlemagne, a war leader who had replaced the Merovingians and was later to style himself Holy Roman Emperor. To further enhance his international status Offa temporarily removed the senior archbishopric of the English Church from Canterbury to his own capital at Lichfield. To this day

Victorian replica effigies of Kent's King Ethelbert and Queen Bertha flank the west front of Lichfield cathedral along with Gregory the Great and Offa himself.

Mercia was not the only rival English kingdom to have an eye on the territory around Canterbury and on the profits to be gained from Kent's close connection to mainland trading systems in Europe. In the ninth century King Alfred of Wessex was another Anglo-Saxon neighbour who aspired to control Kent and the valuable harbours on the shores north, east and south of Canterbury. The expanded writ of 'Saxon' England ran below a line stretching roughly from the Thames estuary to Chester while 'Danish' England controlled the land north of the line. In Canterbury the 'Saxon' age was one of renewed prosperity in farming and in cross-channel trade. As the city once more grew in importance streets such as a new High Street from the St George's Gate to the old West Gate were established. Inside the flint walls land which had once been farmland now acquired a grid of Saxon lanes fronted by workshops and boutiques.

So prosperous did 'Saxon' Canterbury become that the 'Danish' peoples of northern England sent regular raiding parties down to the Kent coast. Each of their shallow-draft, clinker-built, boats was made of oak and pine and needed 20 or 30 men to handle it. The 'Danish' colonies from which the raiding parties came had long been settled by immigrant communities which had taken permanent root in Yorkshire and beyond. Their raiding parties were mounted to seek loot or protection money from Kent. The raids were carried out by 'Vikings' who, according to one etymology, were market raiders who plundered markets called 'wics' in such harbours as 'Ford-Wic' and 'Sand-Wic', Fordwich and Sandwich. It may have been threats from sea robbers which persuaded the nuns of Lyminge to move inland to Canterbury. Some northern raiders set up camp on the islands, Sheppey or Thanet, and even stayed over winter in Kent as in AD 835 or AD 850. One mighty leader of the Viking bands was Olaf, a prince who had been brought up at the Russian court before becoming a sea-robber at the age of eighteen and eventually making himself king of Norway. Canterbury's prosperity, and the related piracy which it encouraged, waned in the last part of the ninth century and for much of the tenth century Canterbury was little disturbed by piratical demands. The end of the tenth century, however, ushered in another twenty years of violent plunder which shook the city to its foundations.

The Viking ogre figures who were used to terrify naughty Canterbury children in the AD 990s came from both the North Sea and the Baltic and included Swedes, Danes, Frisians, Saxons, Norwegians, Russians, Pomeranians and probably many others. Unlike early Scandinavian mariners who had primarily sought warm land on which to settle in the north of England and Ireland as well as Kent, those who came around the year one thousand were concerned with obtaining ready cash which they could take home with them. Their preferred wealth was silver to invest in their pan-European trading activities which eventually stretched down the Volga River to the Black Sea and around the Pillars of Hercules to the Mediterranean lands of the Levant. The money also fertilised the domestic fishing and agriculture of the Scandinavian shorelands. It is not clear how far 'Vikings' visiting Kent took home people as chattels in the way that Norsemen from Iceland did when visiting Ireland in search of fertile young women to populate their remote Atlantic colonies. The most prized source of wealth in Kent was the treasure held in Saxon churches, silver plate and silver communion goblets. Some Saxon churches became fortresses built to protect both material wealth and tithe revenues in coin, and also to protect people who might otherwise be captured for ransom. Churches within sight of the coast sometimes built stone or wooden towers which could serve as look-out posts and signal warnings to the neighbourhood during the summer raiding season.

It was early in the eleventh century that the activities of bands of mercenary war-mongers and piratical ransom-seekers gained a new virulence which threatened Canterbury. One strongman, Thorkill the Mighty, or Thorkill the Tall, commanded a foreign legion of independent marine soldiers with very flexible political allegiances. Over his long career he played off the Danes, Swedes, English, Norwegians and Normans against each other and served whichever of them paid him best. His great raid on Canterbury took place in September of AD 1011. Two years earlier he had allegedly received as 'protection money' a silver payment of £3,000 to persuade him to leave the city in peace. The potential spoils, or ransom payments, were so tempting, however, that he returned with a navy so large, perhaps as many as forty-five ships, that it might have carried 2,000 warriors. These men apparently brought horses with them and were the first cavalry men seen in England to use stirrups to enhance their stability on horseback and improve their military skills. The fleet probably landed its mercenary soldiers on the east coast at Richborough, Sandwich or Walmer, shores previously used by Roman invaders and traders. Smaller Viking ships may have sailed up the Stour to Fordwich a mere two miles below Canterbury.

The history of the siege of Canterbury is full of mysteries and contradictions. The oldest of the monastic houses was St Augustine's, a house which had by now become famous for its Saxon scriptorium where some of the finest and most costly of Europe's manuscripts had been illuminated. The abbey grounds, however, were not particularly well fortified and lay, moreover, outside the circumference of the city wall. It might have been thought that this Benedictine house would have been the obvious target for a large raiding party seeking either protection money or loot. One of the finest books ever made in England was the Golden Codex, prob-ably made in Canterbury and now treasured in a Swedish museum. Jewell-encrusted book covers would have been a tempting target but Abbot Alfmar played a canny game and there is no evidence of damage being done to his abbey during Thorkill's great raid. Indeed abbey life continued as before, and although the skilled work of illu-minating manuscripts may have declined after the Viking visitation, monastic work did not cease and St Augustine's fortunes actually

The illuminated *Codex Aureus* (the Golden Book) may have been crafted in Canterbury but was later seized by Viking raiders. It was recovered and presented to Christ Church in the ninth century. It is now in the National Museum of Sweden. Reproduction: National Library of Sweden.

rose with the acquisition of new landed estates from institutions less fortunate. Thorkill and his men concentrated meanwhile on trying to get into the city whose old wall had been seriously patched up during two decades of 'troubles'. The Vikings were seeking payment from the archbishop, from the cathedral, and from Christ Church Priory.

The September siege lasted for nearly three weeks. St Augustine's Abbey apparently provided the invaders with food, drink and accommodation for themselves and their horses in order to win immunity. The raiding men must, however, have become very impatient to obtain their city spoils and return to their ships and homes before the weather broke and winter set in. After three weeks they had no doubt made serious predatory in-roads into the provisions of the Canterbury suburbs around the street markets of St Dunstan, Wincheap and Longport. On 29 September they finally gained entry to the city itself. It was alleged by some of the spin-doctors of later years that they had threatened to loot St Augustine's Abbey, which was hosting them, if Abbot Alfmar did not secure for them an open gateway to the city. There had rarely been much love lost between the two great monastic houses of Canterbury and siding with one enemy to get the better of another was not unknown. An alternative to such a treasonable explanation for the Viking entry into the city was that they had succeeded in shooting flaming torches over the high walls and had set fire to so many thatched houses that the inhabitants had to flee from the inhalation of smoke. Archaeological evidence for any particular widespread fire is missing, though fire was a regular hazard in any wooden town of the eleventh century. The 'ravaging' of Canterbury did not, however, yield the income that was sought by the invaders. It was alleged that they wanted £48,000 as compared to the £3,000 that had been gained two years earlier. The chroniclers claimed that they set about destroying the town, even the cathedral, in despair or revenge, but the evidence for such destruction is weak. What they did do was take Archbishop Alphege as hostage while the church and city tried

The Saxon craftsmen and needlewomen of Canterbury embroidered the fringe of the Bayeux Tapestry with images of their farming life. © Reading Museum (Reading Borough Council).

to raise the required weight of silver to obtain his freedom. The population which had not been killed by resisting returned to the city from its hiding places in the woods. Seventy year later, when the Domesday survey was undertaken, the city had so revived that the

450 households which owed allegiance to the new Norman king may have numbered 6,000 people.

Alphege was the third archbishop of King Ethelred, the ill-advised and unready king of southern England, to have been approached for Viking protection money. The treasury was probably genuinely short of the funds necessary to pay but the archbishop may, or so his hagiographers claim, have been reluctant to authorise a ransom knowing that if he did so Viking demands would simply go on escalating year on year. Thorkill's men were confident, however, that Alphege would pay in the end and so took him to their war camp at Greenwich and kept him under house arrest for the next six months. They may have also taken other hostages from Canterbury including the abbess of Minster-in-Thanet who had been on a visit to the city when the siege began. She too would have carefully considered the wisdom or otherwise of authorising the payment of ransom money to protect her religious house and its nuns from being robbed or raped. By the spring of 1012, however, no adequate payment had been offered for Alphege. In April he was killed and two quite incompatible accounts of his killing were recorded over the years as he rose to sainthood. One was that officers in Thorkill's army lost patience and killed the archbishop as a sign that they were in earnest and that anyone else who delayed payment might also meet a violent end. But killing the goose that laid the silver eggs would not have been a very clever policy. The alternative account of Alphege's death suggests that he was at a banqueting table with his captors and that they were washing down their ox meat with quantities of ale. When very merry they thought it would be fun to hurl knuckle bones at the archbishop sitting at the top table. Their aim, in spite of their inebriation, was lucky and Alphege was badly injured. Thorkill was unable to save the life of his most valuable asset. There may even have been a mercy killing with an axe to save the priest from an agonisingly protracted death.

The sequel to the death of Alphege brought the Scandinavians back into Canterbury politics. Ethelred, King of England, and Swejn, King of Sweden, both died and their two kingdoms were taken over for the next thirty years by King Cnut who was the son of Swejn but also the husband of Ethelred's Norman widow. The church had rapidly bounced back to life after the dark hiccup of Alphege's death and Christ Church became a particularly successful centre of devotion and learning, even eclipsing St Augustine's. The city rose like a phoenix and new churches were built at St Mildred's, St Dunstan's and St Paul's. In order to show his moral worth, and convert some

Vikings, including members of his court, from Nordic paganism to western Christianity, King Cnut allowed the bones of Alphege to be translated from his tomb in St Paul's at London to a shrine in the cathedral at Canterbury. A martyred archbishop gave a great fillip to the pilgrim trade which, since the days of St Dunstan, had enhanced the wealth of Canterbury. Two hundred years later the pilgrim trade snowballed yet further when another martyred archbishop, Thomas Becket, was given a shrine in the cathedral. Meanwhile Canterbury had thrived before a new wave of Norsemen, this time ones who had been settled in France for the past hundred years, led a new invasion. The Norman Conquest, like the Viking siege, brought trauma to some but status to others who acclaimed the arrival of Duke William from Hastings.

The six centuries of Nordic influence in Canterbury, like the four preceding centuries of Roman influence, brought change to every aspect of the life of the original inhabitants of Kent. These changes brought not only trade and prosperity but also art and literature. In literature Canterbury became, and remained, renowned for its illuminated manuscripts. The finest example of Anglo-Saxon graphic art was the world's most complete and complex 'tapestry', made by calligraphers and needlewomen in Canterbury. The embroidery was commissioned by the newly arrived Normans and illustrates not only the high-living way of life of the aristocracies of 1066 on both sides of the Channel, but also the daily pleasures and penances of the local Kentish peasantry. When completed all seventy panels of this gloriously colourful Canterbury work of art were taken to France and exhibited in the Norman cathedral at Bayeux where they can still be endlessly admired in a purpose-built museum. An equally lasting survival from the Nordic age in the life of Canterbury was religion. When Christianity spread across Europe it often chose a prestigious Roman city as an appropriate seat for a bishop. In matters of religion Canterbury eclipsed London to become the permanent headquarters of the Christian church in England, the seat of a metropolitan bishop who became archbishop and primate. The path had not always been smooth, especially when ecclesiastical wealth attracted Norse pirates, but the status of Canterbury survived even the radical transformations which the French Normans brought to other aspects of English life. The invaders celebrated their arrival by bringing from Normandy all the stone necessary to rebuild the city's soaring cathedral which a thousand years of care and restoration have made one of the jewels of Britain.

Further Reading

IN ADDITION to the annual reports, the quarterly newsletters, and the monographs of the Canterbury Archaeological Trust a number of other books cast direct or indirect light on the early history of Canterbury and its region.

Allason-Jones, Lindsay, *Roman Woman: Everyday Life in Hadrian's Britain* (Michael O'Mara Books, London, 2000)

Ashbee, Paul, *Kent in Prehistoric Times* (Tempus, Stroud, 2005)

Bennett, Paul, Peter Couldrey and Nigel Macpherson-Grant, *Highstead* (C.A.T.New Series, volume IV, Canterbury, 1988)

Berresford Ellis, Peter, *The Ancient World of the Celts* (Constable, London, 1988)

Brookes, Stuart and Sue Harrington, *The Kingdom and People of Kent* (The History Press, Stroud, 2010)

Clarke, Peter, 'The Bronze Age Boat', CAT annual report 2000–2001 (Canterbury, 2003)

Crace, Jim, T*he Gift of Stones* (Penguin, London, 1988)

Detsicas, Alec, *The Cantiaci* (Stutton, Gloucester, 1983)

Eales, Richard, and Richard Gameson, *Vikings, Monks and the Millennium: Canterbury in about 1000 AD* (Canterbury Archaeological Society, 2000)

Everitt, A.M., *Continuity and Colonisation: the evolution of Kentish settlement* (Leicester University Press, 1986)

Foster, Robert (ed.), *The Blean: The Woodlands of a Cathedral City* (Sawd Books, Sittingbourne, 2008)

Jenkins, Frank, *Roman Kent* (Canterbury Archaeological Society, 1966)

Jessup, Frank W., *Kent History Illustrated* (Kent County Council, 1966)

Lincoln, E.F., *The Story of Canterbury* (Staples, London, 1955)

Lyle, Marjorie, *Seven Buried Canterbury Tales* (Marjorie Lyle, Canterbury, 1996)

Peddie, John, *Conquest: The Roman Invasion of Britain* (Sutton, Stroud, 1987)

Pepper, Ron, 'Bigbury' in *Harbledown Heritage* (Harbledown Conservation Association, 2000)

Tatton-Brown, Tim, *Canterbury* (Sutton, Stroud, 1994)

Trevor, Meriol, *The New People* (Macmillan, London, 1957)

Williams, John H. (ed.), *The Archaeology of Kent to AD 800* (The Boydell Press,Woodbridge, 2007)

Witney, K.P., *The Jutish Forest from 450 to 1300 AD* (Athlone, London, 1976)

Witney, K.P., *The Kingdom of Kent* (Phillimore, 1983)